The All-in-One College Guide

Second Edition

Marty Nemko, Ph.D.

BARRON'S

All inquiries should be addressed to:
Barron's Educational Series, Inc.
250 Wireless Boulevard
Hauppauge, New York 11788
http://www.barronseduc.com

ISBN-13: 978-0-7641-2298-9
ISBN-10: 0-7641-2298-3

Library of Congress Catalog Card No.: 2003063897

Library of Congress Cataloging-in-Publication Data
Nemko, Marty, 1945–
        The all-in-one college guide / Marty Nemko.—2nd ed.
                p.   cm.
        ISBN 0-7641-2298-3
        1. College choice—United States. 2. College student orientation—
        United States. I. Title.

  LB2350.5.N467 2004
  378.1'61—dc22   2003063897

PRINTED IN THE UNITED STATES OF AMERICA

9 8 7 6 5 4 3 2

The All-in-One College Guide

Contents

Getting Into Killer Colleges Without Killing Yourself / 43

Finding the Money / 74

The Keys to a Great College Experience / 99

Appendices / 149

Appendix A

Appendix B

About the Author

Dr. Marty Nemko has seen college from all sides:

— **Student:** He holds a Ph.D. in education from the University of California, Berkeley.

— **Professor:** He has taught at four universities, including Berkeley.

— **Counselor:** He has counseled more than 2,000 clients on both college and career choices. He enjoys a 97 percent client satisfaction rate. Prospective clients can e-mail him at *mnemko@earthlink.net*.

— **Consultant:** He has worked with 15 college presidents on how to improve undergraduate education.

— **Writer:** He has written four books. Former U.S. Secretary of Education Terrel Bell called his book *How to Get an Ivy League Education at a State University* "thorough, reliable, and remarkably helpful." A review in the *Los Angeles Times* of his book *Cool Careers for Dummies* said it is "filled with smart ideas." The American School Board Association named his book *How to Get Your Child a Private School Education in a Public School* one of the year's "Ten Must Books." His column appears in the Sunday *San Francisco Chronicle*. More than 400 of his articles and columns are available online at *www.martynemko.com*.

— **Critic.** A tireless advocate for students, he has been interviewed by hundreds of major media outlets. ABC-TV and KCBS called him "The Ralph Nader of Education."

Acknowledgments

Before he died, former U.S. Commissioner of Education Ernest Boyer told me that he wished he could have written a book that told students and parents what they *really* needed to know about college. He said he was glad I was going to write it. This encouragement, from one of America's most respected educators, was a major inspiration.

I equally appreciate my many guinea pigs on whom I tried the ideas in this book: the students of Berkeley and Skyline High Schools, and, of course, my private clients.

Some of the busiest, most talented college counselors on earth took the time to review the manuscript: Steve Antonoff, Marsha Irwin, Mary Jane Kravets, Phyllis Steinbrecher, and Kal Chany. Colleen Rush and Jennifer Trussell added spicy editorial tidbits, and some noneducators helped make sure it all made sense to just plain parents: David Wilens, Ray Mattoon, Barbara Griffith, and Kelly Manzer.

I am thankful for the good people at Barron's, especially Grace Freedson for her open mind and promptness, Max Reed, and Tom Vanderberg who were involved in the production of my original book, and Pat Hunter who worked on this revised edition.

Finally, to my wife, Dr. Barbara Nemko, thank you for tolerating a workaholic husband.

Marty Nemko
Oakland, California

Introduction

Why You Should Read This Book

There's a mountain of college information out there. This book includes only the best of the best. Whether you're an A student or just a student, you'll know

✓ the specific colleges *you* should apply to. You'll develop your custom-tailored list right here in this book. And your list will likely be more on target than a computer-generated list.

✓ how to get in without losing your mind.

✓ how to find the cash to pay for college. Did you know that two families with the same income and assets can get totally different amounts of financial aid from the same college? I'll show you how to get the most money you're legally entitled to.

✓ the keys to a great college experience: How to find the best professors, get good grades, make friends, get along with your roommate, manage your time, and graduate with a good job or get into a good graduate school—having a good time all along the way.

I'll focus on the important information that isn't widely known. For example, do you know

✓ there are easier routes into prestigious colleges (for example, Harvard's evening bachelor's programs)?

✓ whether you'd do better on the SAT or the ACT?

✓ whether you should sign up for an expensive SAT/ACT preparation course?

✓ if it's better to get an A in a regular class or a B in an honors class?

✓ that almost 40 percent of students surveyed at the nation's designer-label colleges believed their college wasn't worth the money? (There may be wiser choices than brand-name schools and I'll tell you about them!)

✓ how to ensure that your essay reveals your best self?

✓ that the college rankings published in major news magazines can be misleading?

✓ that a letter from a college encouraging you to apply does not indicate that it will admit you?

✓ whether you should go straight to college or not? (See page 217.)

✓ how to find the right career for you?

✓ how to pick a major you'll be happy with?

✓ easy ways to meet new friends at college?

I will share all that and much more with you. I've even included crucial ideas for parents that can prevent lots of stress.

Rather than read this book cover to cover, treat it as an encyclopedia: Look up what you need when you need it. When you're ready to choose a college, read that section. When you're ready to think about the SAT, read that section. When you've had enough, slam it shut knowing it is at your service 24/7.

Before we get to Job One (getting you a list of colleges at which you're most likely to be happy and successful), I'd better warn you what not to do. Literally millions of college-bound students have made the following mistakes.

Top Six Mistakes in Choosing a College

6. **Relying on the rankings in major news magazines.** It's absurd, but the rankings are based mainly on data that each college's administration itself submits. That's like *Rolling Stone* asking a singer to review her own CD. Not surprisingly, the *Wall Street Journal* has reported that some colleges fudge the data they submit. And the rankings are based in part on how good the students are. As an article in the November 2003 *Atlantic Monthly* pointed out, "That's like judging the competence of a doctor who only sees robustly healthy patients."

   Even worse, these rankings are created totally without input from the most relevant persons of all: the colleges' students. Who do these magazines poll? College administrators, many of whom have never even visited most of the campuses they're asked to rate! Would you trust a restaurant rating written by a reviewer who had never seen the restaurant, let alone eaten there?

   Big-name undergraduate colleges are not necessarily the best.

5. **Relying on a college's reputation.** Sure, if you're a straight A student with a super SAT score, you might want to consider designer-label colleges like the Ivys or Stanford. After all, they do offer top students great campus resources, a career door-opening name on your diploma, and the great feeling that comes from knowing and being able to tell others that you attend a prestigious college. But even many top students should think twice. Many prestigious colleges get their good reputations because their professors do a lot of research, because the colleges are large, old, and therefore well known, and because of the good jobs many of their graduates get. None of these are great reasons to choose a college. Here's why.

   Professors' research often lowers the quality of undergraduate education. For the $175,000 four-year cost at research universities[1] (for example, Harvard, Yale, and Stanford), there are too many

---

[1] A university basically means a large college that has graduate as well as undergraduate students.

auditorium-sized classes taught by professors who care more about what's in their test tubes than what's in their students' heads.

Large: Bigger often means large classes, more red tape, and less individual attention.

Jobs and graduate schools. Yes, a designer label on a diploma is a plus in the job market. But Ivy-caliber students may get an equal or better advantage if they attend a less prestigious college, because there they are more likely to get top grades, personal attention, leadership opportunities, and superb letters of recommendation.

A Princeton University study compared the lifetime earnings of students who were accepted to designer-label colleges but attended lesser-known schools with the earnings of students who attended the designer-label schools. The two groups earned an equal amount. Why? It's the kids that matter. You could lock the Ivy-admitted into a closet for four years and they'll earn more than non-Ivy students.

Go beyond earning to learning, and brand-name colleges still don't rule. There is no evidence that similar students learn more at prestigious colleges. Loren Pope, author of *Looking Beyond the Ivy League,* lists the 20 colleges with the highest percentage of graduates going on to earn Ph.Ds. Reed College in Oregon, New College in Florida, and Wabash College in Indiana all made the list. Harvard and Yale didn't.

> **Less selective colleges will often give a big scholarship to Ivy-caliber students.**

Also, the pressure cooker environment of designer-label colleges has destroyed many a promising student. Fran Schumer, in *Most Likely to Succeed: Six Women from Harvard and What Became of Them* reported that the anorexia and binge drinking at Harvard was so pervasive that the toilet pipes in the women's dorms had to be replaced each year because they had eroded from all the stomach acid.

My own daughter, who was admitted to Williams College, one of the nation's hardest-to-get-into colleges, instead opted for a less selective one. Because she was able to excel there, she got noticed by her professors, one of whom gave her a tip on a job in the White House. She ended up working for almost a year in Hillary Clinton's research office. Lest you think my daughter is an exception, 40 percent of the nation's CEOs got their undergraduate degrees at public universities. Less selective colleges will often give a big scholarship to Ivy-caliber students.

In short, there's more to consider than just a college's name. I'm not asking you to dismiss designer-label colleges, but it's worth keeping an open mind: learn about the many fine but less well-known colleges I'll tell you about and then decide where to apply.

4. **Assuming more costly colleges are better.** Public colleges are subsidized by your tax dollars so their price is lower. It doesn't mean their quality is lower.

3. **Relying on one person's opinion** (for example, your girlfriend, your uncle, or even your parent). The best decisions are usually made when you gather information from multiple sources. (I'll clue you in on easy ways to get the info you need. See Chapter 2.)

2. **Being too shy to ask questions.** You're buying an expensive product that will take four to six years of your life. You have the right to ask questions. Representatives from the colleges love to answer questions and so do college students. If someone was thinking of attending your high school and asked how you like it, wouldn't you tell the person? Don't know what to ask? Questions that would make Sherlock Holmes proud are on pp. 30–32.

> **The amount of attention you get while a college is recruiting you does not indicate how much attention you'll get after you're enrolled at the college.**

1. **Relying on a college's advertising:** campus tours, campus representatives visiting your high school, the stuff that fills your mailbox and e-mailbox, interviews (yes, these too are advertising), get-togethers for admitted students, open houses, and handwritten

notes or phone calls from a student or professor at the college. A few colleges even send top students an individualized video from the college president: "Hi, Mary. I'm really hoping you'll join us this fall."

Statistics trumpeted by the college are also advertising. For example, many brand-name universities report a faculty/student ratio of less than 20:1 even though the typical undergraduate spends much time in classes of 100+. How do colleges get away with it? They count classes you'll probably never take, for example, Advanced Sanskrit, and classes for Ph.D. students. They may even count professors who never teach anyone—they only do research. Remember, colleges are a business much like any other business. To sell, many colleges hide their negatives, stretch their positives, and as mentioned above, may even distort the truth.

Unfortunately, you must think of admissions representatives as salespersons, not as admissions counselors, which is what they like to call themselves. You may think I'm being harsh, but the fact is, admissions "counselors" rarely counsel a student not to apply. Too few are likely to say, for example, what a true counselor might: "I'm not sure this college is challenging enough for you. Why not apply to more selective colleges?" Admissions reps' job is to sell their college.[2]

Now here's the right way to choose a college.

---

[2] Questionable admissions practices are described in more detail in "Deny the Brutes," by Thomas Sturgeon, associate director of admission at Duke. *Journal of College Admission,* June 1995, pp. 16–23.

1
The Sagas of Mary and Sandy
(based on true stories)

Misguided Mary

The daughter of a friend—I'll call her, Misguided Mary—had always dreamed of attending a designer-label college. Her parents shared her dream. After all, it would open all those career doors, and besides, it would be cool to have that Harvard decal on their car's rear window.

By the time Mary started the ninth grade, her parents had already hired an expensive college consultant. The consultant recommended that to maximize Mary's chances of admission to a designer-label college, she needed to take six solids and as many honors and especially Advanced Placement courses as possible.

Sometimes Mary would cry, overwhelmed with all the work, and she always had to scramble to get it all done. Much of what she crammed in, she forgot soon after the test.

The consultant told her not to dabble but to focus on one extracurricular—that impresses the colleges. The consultant recommended lacrosse, because even designer-label colleges are usually short of students who can play a minor sport.

Mary spent her summers at lacrosse camp. Not surprisingly, all the lacrosse practices and games on top of six hard solids left little time for relaxing and just being a teenager.

She took the PSAT as a sophomore and got "only" a 1270* (better than 87 percent of students who took the test). That scared her because the profiles for students admitted to institutions such as Harvard and Stanford

---

*Note: As of March 2005, the SAT will have a maximum score of 2400 instead of 1600.

suggested that she needed around 1400. So, in the fall of her junior year, she enrolled in one of those $900 SAT prep courses. That swallowed up even more time: the time it took to get driven to and from the class, the class time, and the nightly SAT-prep homework assignments.

Because SAT prep demanded all that time, her GPA declined slightly: from 3.9 before the SAT, down to a 3.7. This is ironic, because grades count much more than SAT scores in college admissions.

When Mary took the SAT in March of her junior year, she was understandably stressed, not only from her heavy load, but because of the pressure from friends, parents, and herself to do well on the test. She felt her future hung on how well she did. Not surprisingly, despite the prep course, her score increased only 20 points to 1290. (Small increases are quite common.)

In the summer of her junior year, she spent part of the summer at Harvard Summer School ($6,200) even though she was sick of school. Her consultant suggested, "It couldn't hurt to show more commitment."

Mary started her senior year stressed out and burned out, but again taking six solids, including two honors and two Advanced Placement courses, plus lacrosse, plus studying one more time for the SAT. Her score increased to 1350, and she was delighted.

Mary was scared that nonetheless, her profile was marginal for a designer-label school. So she decided to give herself an edge: she'd apply somewhere Early Decision. Her consultant explained that Stanford and Harvard were not realistic, but that she had a shot at another Ivy League school—the University of Pennsylvania, especially if she applied Early Decision, because Penn takes almost 40 percent of its class Early Decision. The clincher was that Penn's business major is among the most prestigious.

Mary got into Penn, and everyone was thrilled—until they saw her financial aid package. Early Decision students often get a bad package because the colleges don't have to worry about competing colleges. Of the $175,000 four-year price tag, her parents would have to come up with $100,000 in cash and take $30,000 in loans, and Mary would have to hold a part-time job throughout her four years. Mary's parents didn't want to deny their child their long-standing dream, so they said they'd pay.

In early April, Mary flew from her home in California to Penn's "party" for accepted students. Not unusual, there was a late cold snap—

Mary, who had lived in California all her life, hadn't realized how cold cold can be. She also hadn't realized how different the students are in the East: more aggressive, more formal. Mary started to feel nervous about her decision to attend Penn, but having applied Early Decision, she didn't have a choice—she was required to attend.

Not surprisingly, when Mary arrived at Penn to start school, she was more burned out on academics than excited. She was also glad to get away from the pressure of her parents, and nervous about whether she was smart enough to be at an Ivy League school. That bad combination led her to a freshman year noted more by partying than by studying. The result was a 2.4 GPA.

At the beginning of her sophomore year, she applied to be a business major, but because of her freshman-year GPA, she was rejected. She decided to major in what she thought was a similar major, economics, but the more she got into the major, the more she realized the economics major consisted mostly of math—not her strength, nor her interest.

Mary decided to struggle through the econ major because starting another one would delay her graduation at least a semester and cost her family at least $20,000 extra.

She graduated, but with only a 2.7 and the feeling that she was hardly an expert on economics, especially compared with her Ivy League peers.

Nonetheless she figured that a degree from Penn would open career doors. After more effort than she anticipated, she landed a position as an analyst for a financial services firm in Philadelphia. She had not intended to live in the East, but most of the on-campus recruited jobs were in the same region as Penn.

Mary arrived at her job with a $29,000 loan to repay and a bad case of the imposter syndrome. The Ivy League name on her diploma didn't begin to boost her self-esteem.

Savvy Sandy

Like Mary, Savvy Sandy was attracted to designer-label colleges, but for the right reason. She knew she'd thrive best when her classmates were tops. But Sandy was committed to doing only things that would help her grow or give her pleasure, not just impress a college admissions committee.

So she took five, not six, solids per semester. And she didn't reflexively choose the honors or AP course. She decided based on how good the teacher was, whether she was interested enough in the subject to want to spend more time studying it, how hard the rest of her program was, and how time-consuming her extracurriculars would be. Sandy took some honors and AP courses but only half as many as Mary. This allowed her time to have a social life and to breathe.

In her extracurriculars, Sandy wanted to dabble even if it wouldn't impress the college admissions committee. She took a photography class and a papermaking class, tried out for cheerleading, wrote some poetry, and went on a Christmas trip to Costa Rica.

By her junior year, she found that she most enjoyed writing. Little by little, she did more: some more poems, then an occasional article for the student newspaper. She even submitted an article to the *San Francisco Chronicle*. But she always stayed in balance: moderate studying, moderate social life, a variety of extracurriculars. She was able to get a 3.9 with a moderate amount of study.

Sandy took the PSAT not in her sophomore year, but in October of her junior year and got the same 1270 Mary did. Instead of signing up for a $900 SAT course, six weeks before the May administration, she spent 15 minutes a few nights a week with the $25 Inside the SAT/ACT software program.

Sandy ended up with a 1320 on the SAT. She realized that retaking it would require more time and more studying, taking more time away from her studying for school grades, which count more than the SAT score. So 1320 was it. (That, of course, was higher than 92% of all students who took the test!)

As Sandy began her senior year, she realized that because she had not been an extracurricular star and because she had scored "only" 1320 on the SAT, she probably was not going to get into a Harvard or Stanford.

She decided that schools like Penn probably weren't worth it. She did a little homework and found out that because her parents, like Mary's, earned $90,000, her family would be jeopardizing their financial security to pay for a brand-name private college.

So Sandy decided to apply to four of the public universities in California, any of which would cost her family 50 percent less. Her top choices were Berkeley and UCLA, not just because of their prestige, but because she knew she'd do better with bright classmates. Her backup schools were the University of California at Davis and the University of California at Santa Cruz.

Surprised, she was admitted only to Davis and Santa Cruz. As balanced as her attitude had been, this saddened her more than she had anticipated.

She was about to turn in her letter of intent to attend Davis when she heard that a surprising number of even outstanding high school graduates take an interim year: a series of interesting nonacademic experiences. Many private colleges, including Harvard, encourage students to do this. Unfortunately, the University of California requires students to reapply. But because Sandy wasn't thrilled with the idea of going to Davis and was ready for a break from academics, she figured she'd take the risk. She had heard that with a year's worth of interesting experiences to write about in her admission essay, her application might be seen more favorably.

She spent the year in the Leap Now program, which allowed her to do adventure travel in Nepal, volunteer work in South America, and three mini-internships in the United States. Those experiences were impressive in her college applications and not surprisingly, she was admitted to the University of California at San Diego.

Now refreshed, Sandy, unlike Mary, was ready to make the most of college. To avoid the megalecture classes, she signed up for the special freshman seminars. She volunteered to do research for a professor she liked. She asked another of her favorite professors to guide her in an independent study of Panama. Those experiences yielded great recommendations, so she landed, in her junior year, an internship at the Agency for International Development.

Despite not having an Ivy League degree, she had acquired more people skills by having lived a balanced life, which impressed her colleagues at AID. That, plus her high school trip to Costa Rica, her independent study on Panama, and Leap Now interim year, meant that, when a paying job opened at AID after she graduated, she got it. Sandy now works on assisting U.S. physicians going to rural Central and South America to train locals to be medics.

Importantly, Sandy's self-esteem is far stronger because it is based not on a designer label on her diploma but on what she has accomplished.

2

Here Is Your Personalized List of Colleges

What I Want in a College

Directions: You'll end up with a better list of colleges if you and your parent(s) answer these questions together. Or do it solo and then see if your parents agree with your choices.

I'm willing to consider colleges that are

1. **(Circle one or both)**

   two-year

   four-year

   (Want help deciding? See p. 149.)

   Note: Many good students might consider starting at a two-year college.

2. filled with students who in high school were
   (Choose one)

   A students (1250–1600 on old SAT, 1900–2400 on new SAT, or 28–36 on ACT)

   B to A students (1050–1250 on old SAT, 1600–1875 on new SAT, or 22–27 on ACT)

   B students, but the colleges have honors programs to challenge A students

B– to C+ students (900–1100 on old SAT, 1350–1650 on new SAT, or 18–21 on ACT)

(Want help deciding? See p. 152.)

3. priced for four years, not counting financial aid, at \$_____or less.

Here's a rough estimate of total costs including living expenses and not counting financial aid for four years of college:

✓ Brand-name private colleges: \$175,000

✓ Less well-known private colleges, for example, Creighton, Millsaps, Hillsdale: \$120,000

✓ Brand-name public colleges and those in high-cost states, for example, Berkeley, Michigan, SUNY-Binghamton: \$80,000 in-state (\$125,000 out-of-state)

✓ Less-well known public colleges in low-cost states, for example, Truman State, North Carolina-Asheville, most two-year public colleges: \$40,000–60,000.
(Want help deciding? See p. 76 and p. 157.)

4. (Circle one or more)

small

large

have a living/learning program (sort of like a small college within a large one)

(Want help deciding? See p. 158.)

5. (Circle one or more)

in/near a big city

away from a big city

(Want help deciding? See p. 161.)

6. in specific state(s) or city(ies):_____

in specific regions:

(Circle one or more)

Northeast

South

Midwest

West

(Want help deciding? See p. 161.)

7. (Circle one or both)

offer many majors

that specialize

(Want help deciding? See p. 162.)

8. (Circle one or more)

conservative/traditional

moderate/diverse

liberal/unconventional

(Want help deciding? See p. 162.)

9. (Circle one or more)

mixed gender and race

single gender

single race

(Want help deciding? See p. 163.)

10. (Circle one or both)

secular or not strongly religious

strongly religious

(Want help deciding? See p. 164.)

11. offer an academic calendar of
(Circle one or more)

quarters

semesters

4-1-4

block

(Want help deciding? See p. 165.)

12. Would you like a college that offers a co-op program?
If so, circle this: *yes*

(Want help deciding? See p. 166.)

13. Would you like a college that offers extensive disability services?
If so, circle this: *yes*

(Want help deciding? See p. 166.)

Now, look over all the items you circled and put a star next to the few items you *most* want in your college.

IMPORTANT DIRECTIONS!

(They're simpler to follow than they look.)

It's impossible to look carefully at all of the nation's 3,500 colleges. So, first you have to decide on a manageable number (10–15) of colleges to consider that are potentially right for *you*. Here's how to do it quickly:

Step 1. Write down the names of any colleges you already know you want to consider. Maybe it's the college you've been dreaming about since preschool, the one your coach recommended or a parent attended, or a local college that fits what you circled on your *What I Want* list.

Step 2. Mark an X next to the **categories** below that fit the *What I Want* list you just created. Select enough categories so you have 20–30 colleges to choose from.

CATEGORIES

Two-Year Colleges

Northeast (10 of these colleges are on p. 168)
South (1 of these is on p. 168)
Midwest (5 of these are on pp. 168–169)
West (4 of these are on p. 169)

Four-Year Colleges Offering Many Majors

Mainly A Students

Small, Northeast, in/near big city (6 of these are on p. 169)
Small, Northeast, town (6 of these are on p. 169)
Small, South, in/near big city (1 of these is on p. 169)
Small, South, town (1 of these is on p. 170)
Small, Midwest, in/near big city (1 of these is on p. 170)
Small, Midwest, town (2 of these are on p. 170)
Small, West, in/near big city (3 of these are on p. 170)
Small, West, town (1 of these is on p. 170)

Large, Northeast, in/near big city (8 of these are on p. 170)
Large, Northeast, town (2 of these are on p. 170)
Large, South, in/near big city (1 of these is on p. 171)
Large, South, town (1 of these is on p. 171)
Large, Midwest, in/near big city (1 of these is on p. 171)
Large, Midwest, town (1 of these is on p. 171)
Large, West, in/near big city (3 of these are on p. 171)

Mainly B to A Students

Small, Northeast, in/near big city (6 of these are on p. 171)
Small, Northeast, town (16 of these are on pp. 171–172)
Small, South, in/near big city (5 of these are on p. 172)
Small, South, town (3 of these are on p. 172)
Small, Midwest, in/near big city (3 of these are on p. 172)
Small, Midwest, town (3 of these are on p. 173)
Small, West, in/near big city (1 of these is on p. 173)

Large, Northeast, in/near big city (9 of these are on p. 173)
Large, Northeast, town (6 of these are on pp. 173–174)

Large, South, in/near big city (5 of these are on p. 174)
Large, South, town (1 of these is on p. 174)
Large, Midwest, in/near big city (3 of these are on p. 174)
Large, Midwest, town (2 of these are on p. 174)
Large, West, in/near big city (1 of these is on p. 174)
Large, West, town (2 of these are on p. 174)

Many B– Students

Small, Northeast, in/near big city (16 of these are on pp. 174–175)
Small, Northeast, town (31 of these are on pp. 175–176)
Small, South, in/near big city (21 of these are on pp. 176–177)
Small, South, town (22 of these are on pp. 177–178)
Small, Midwest, in/near big city (15 of these are on p. 178)
Small, Midwest, town (38 of these are on pp. 178–179)
Small, West, in/near big city (15 of these are on p. 180)
Small, West, town (11 of these are on p. 180)

Large, Northeast, in/near big city (12 of these are on p. 181)
Large, Northeast, town (10 of these are on p. 181)
Large, South, in/near big city (12 of these are on p. 182)
Large, South, town (12 of these are on p. 182)
Large, Midwest, in/near big city (21 of these are on p. 183)
Large, Midwest, town (6 of these are on p. 183)
Large, West, in/near big city (12 of these are on p. 184)
Large, West, town (9 of these are on pp. 184)

Four-Year Colleges That Specialize

Military (5 of these are on p. 185)
Engineering & Physical Sciences (15 of these are on pp. 185–186)
Business (3 of these are on p. 186)
Visual Arts (10 of these are on pp. 186–187)
Performing Arts (12 of these are on p. 187)

Step 3. Turn to the page listed for each category you've just chosen. Use the information provided there about each college to narrow your list to 10–15 colleges. If you know you'll want an unusual major or sport, narrow to 15–20 colleges rather than 10–15.

Step 4. If you have a college counselor, get his or her reaction to your list. You might cross-check your list against the one generated for you at *princetonreview.com*. Click on "college," then on "Counselor-O-Matic." It also has an online forum on which counselors may help you whittle your list.

Step 5. To find out which of your selected colleges actually fit you and are of high quality, turn to page 13.

3
From Initial List to Final Choice

"For all but about 150 (of the nation's 4,000 colleges), selectivity is out the window. Today, 91% of students are accepted by one of their two college choices."

Anna Leider, author of Don't Miss Out

Presto, change-o, in Chapter 2 you narrowed your search from 4,000 to 10 to 15 colleges. Now here's how to further pare down your list to the 3 to 10 you'll actually apply to.

First, an Insider's Secret

Ninety-five percent of colleges need you more than you need them. Why? Because, believe it or not, most colleges never fill all their slots. If you enroll, that's money they wouldn't otherwise have.

Moral of the story: Be picky. Choosing a college is like buying clothes. There are hundreds of garments to choose from.

If in September, you called colleges and said, "I'd like to start next week but can only afford half of your tuition," many good colleges would say, "Send in an application and we'll see what we can do."

You're trying to figure out which give you the best quality and fit for the money. This chapter tells you how to do it.

Step 1: Keep a College Notebook

Take a section of your school notebook with 10 to 15 pages, and label it "colleges." Then write the names of the 10 to 15 colleges on your list, one on the top of each page.

Step 2: Find Clues on the Net

Find out which of the 10 to 15 colleges on your list offer your desired major(s), sport, honors program, and so on. How do you find out? Just go to each college's web site. Don't know its web address? Go to *www.google.com* and search on the college's name.

If a college doesn't offer your major, sport, or an honors program, note that in your college notebook, or even cross the college off your list. Warning to athletes: Unless you're a true pro prospect, be sure to choose a college first because it's a good fit academically and socially, and second because you'd enjoy playing sports there.

You might be saying, "But I don't know what I want to major in." Not to worry. I'll show you how to find the right major and a well-suited career in Appendix E. (Those pages may be the most useful in this entire book, pp. 195–216.)

By the way, most colleges' web sites are filled with all sorts of other information: everything that's in its catalog, homepages of campus student groups, campus event schedules, photographs of the campus, copies of the campus newspaper, and maybe student evaluations of courses or a campus directory so you can e-mail questions to students, faculty, and coaches. Great source!

INSIDER'S SECRET Here is how the pros get the most valid information about a college.

✓ Review the college's latest student satisfaction survey. If an unedited copy isn't on the college's web site, request it from the president's office. (If the college says it doesn't make it public, beware.)

✓ Read the report from the last accreditation team's visit. If an unedited version is not posted on the college's web site, request it from the president's office. (If the college says it's not available to the public, beware.)

If you want the inside story on a college, check out its student newspaper online; or if it's not online, call the college and ask the student newspaper office to mail you a few copies. College newspapers from all around the nation are available at:

yahoo.com/News_ and_Media/Newspapers/College_and_University
http://beacon-www.asa.utk.edu/resources/papers.html

Other things to check out on the site:

✓ Have you taken the high school courses and exams that the college requires?

✓ Are there enough professors in your intended major? The more there are to choose from, the easier it will be to find good ones, and to have plenty of course choices.

✓ Do the college courses in your prospective major sound interesting?

✓ Are there special programs that intrigue you? For example, a combination biology and business major?

✓ Does the college require you to take too many college courses you'd hate to take, either for your major or as a general graduation requirement? Can you handle calculus? More foreign language?

✓ How much credit toward your college degree will you get for your Advanced Placement or International Baccalaureate courses?

Step 3: Read About Your Colleges in a Guide That Reports Student Opinions

This may be the smartest way to judge a college's quality and fit.

✓ *The Best 357 Colleges* offers a two-page writeup that distills what more than 100 randomly selected students think of their college.

✓ *The Fiske Guide to Colleges* offers three- to four-page essays on 330 colleges based on a small number of student questionnaires and one submitted by an administrator. These essays offer different information: strong majors, special programs, details about out-of-class life, and a description of the physical campus and surroundings.

✓ *Barron's Guide to the Most Competitive Colleges* offers a 10–15 page essay on each of 65 hard-to-get-into colleges, written by one student or recent alum.

✓ *Barron's Best Buys in College Education* offers profiles of 300 well-priced colleges that meld student opinion with useful statistics. Another plus is that it covers many colleges not profiled in other guides.

In the latter three guides, you won't find much negative information about any college because the queried students were hand-picked by each college's administration.

You can uncover a college's negative aspects by asking good questions of students during your virtual and actual visits. See pages 17–19 and 22–34.

Even *The Best 357 Colleges*, which surveys students virtually at random, can occasionally present an overly positive picture of a college. For

> **If you simply choose 3 to 10 favorite colleges to apply to based on Steps 1 to 3, you've done a better job of choosing than most students.**

example, at a major state university, a few days before the surveyors from *The Best 357 Colleges* were coming on campus to poll the students, the college's administration launched a campaign to let students know how important it was that the college came out looking good.

IMPORTANT! This may seem odd, but throughout your college search, focus on the negative. Colleges will take care of presenting the positive. You'll soon notice that all brochures show picture-perfect weather and classes with no more than ten fascinated students. Yeah, right.

Step 4: Rent the Video

Don't give too much weight to the videos that the colleges send to you or the video clips on colleges' web sites. Those are commercials made by the colleges. The colleges spend big bucks to hire slick advertising firms to make those videos as seductive as possible. Watch them and you may end up choosing the best commercial rather than the best college.

The videos most worth watching are put out by a dedicated college counselor named Cliff Kramon. He visited 350 colleges, from Oxford in England to Harvey Mudd in California. With camcorder in hand, he simply took each college's tour and recorded it along with the questions he and others asked of the tour guide. You and as many family members and friends as you like get to tour as many colleges as you want, no matter how far away, in the comfort of your living room for just $15 a piece, the price of two movie tickets. If you're on a budget, rent videos only of colleges that you're thinking of dropping from your list. Order at *www.collegiatechoice.com*. That site also has humorist Dave Barry's take on college. It's the funniest thing I've read on campus life.

Step 5: Make a Virtual Visit

In a virtual visit, you get to talk with the college's students without having to leave home.

Is this helpful? You betcha. You get personalized answers to your questions from random students rather than from college reps whose job is to sell the college to you. If you were about to buy a car, wouldn't you want to talk with someone who owns the same car, not just the salesperson? Students are in the best position to describe what student life on campus is really like.

You may fear you're imposing. You're not. Imagine that a student who was thinking of attending your high school asked what you thought of your school. Wouldn't you be willing to talk?

Don't worry, you won't seem geeky. Just think of it as sampling the goods before you buy.

How to get to talk with students? Easy. No need to trek all the way to campus. No matter which college, there's a supply of students just a phone call or e-mail away. Maybe you know a friend or relative at the college. Or perhaps your high school keeps a list of former students and the colleges they attend. Or see if the college's web site allows you to e-mail students there or has links to students' home pages. That's a great option if you're shy. Or contact an alumnus. Alumni are a great source of info about a college. They've spent years there and have the benefit of hindsight. Focus on recent graduates. Colleges change (slowly). There's a list of alumni of most colleges at *www.alumni.net.*

None of the above sound good? No problem. You can conduct your virtual visit on the phone. Just muster a little courage, phone the college switchboard (phone numbers for 434 colleges that draw a nonlocal student body are on pp. 168–187) and ask to have the call transferred to a residence hall front desk. Most dorms have a student there to answer the phone.

To start the conversation, try something like, "Hi, I'm a high school student who is thinking about attending your college. I've read about it, but I thought I'd learn more by talking with some students. Do you like it?" Take notes. Ask a few other questions (see list on pp. 30–32), then ask if another student is around. If not, have the call transferred to another dorm, to the student government office, or student newspaper office. Don't get too swayed by a single student who either loves or hates the college.

You might also contact the department you're planning to major in. Explain that you're shopping for a college. Then ask if there's anything about the undergraduate program you should know that isn't in the catalog. That information might help you decide if that college is a good choice for you. You can then cite that information in your admission essay: "Happy Days College is a particularly good fit for me because I'm planning to major in psychology and your department specializes in physiological psychology, which is my main interest." If you're really lucky, your call to the department can even result in your contact putting a good word in for you with the admissions office—after all, you were motivated enough to check out the department, something that 99 percent of applicants aren't.

A PATCH OF IVY?

If you're interested in an honors program, call the switchboard and ask to be transferred to the honors office. Ask five questions: how many honors classes are offered each term? What out-of-classroom opportunities are there for students in the honors programs? Is there an honors residence hall? Do honors students get special privileges such as first crack at course registration? What does it take to get admitted to the program?

If after your virtual visit, you're still interested in the college, have the call transferred to the admissions office. Ask a few questions. (Or ask them on the college's web site.)

My favorite questions for admission counselors (salespeople):

✓ How is this college different from other small (or large) rural (or urban) colleges?

✓ Are there any special programs or opportunities that help a student to have a particularly rewarding experience compared with other colleges?

✓ What percentage of students with my SAT/ACT score and high school grades graduate from your college within four years? Five years?

✓ What are students' most legitimate gripes about the college?

Again, if you're feeling too shy to ask, remember that the college isn't too shy to ask for your

Remember: at 95 percent of colleges, they need you more than you need them.

$50,000 to $175,000 and four or more years of your life. You're entitled to quality information before buying. Don't be in awe of colleges. Remember, they are a business, and you're the customer they're trying to sell to. They don't want you to think that. They want you to think that slots at the college are hard to come by and you'd be lucky to get one. The fact is, it's the opposite.

Step 6: Apply to the Colleges

At this point, you probably have enough information to determine which 3 to 10 colleges to apply to. If you'd like even more information, do Step 8 and/or 9.

It's safest and easiest to apply online, right at each college's web site. In addition to your application for admission, apply for financial aid, even if your family is well off. Unless you do, you may not be considered for merit-based aid (how smart and talented you are). Check to see whether you need to apply for housing now or after you're admitted.

Visit *commonapp.org* to see if you can use the Common Application. Two hundred fifty selective colleges allow it, and treat it like their own application. Use that and you have to enter your information one time, and may be able to write one essay for any of the 250 to which you apply.

HOW MANY COLLEGES SHOULD YOU APPLY TO?

Many students apply to too few colleges. One reason to apply to more is that it can help you negotiate: "I'd like to come to your college, but it's just too expensive. FatCat College offered me $5,000 more financial aid." Yes, often you can negotiate financial aid.

And remember, it may not be much more work to crank out a few more applications. An essay for one college can often be used for another. Also, as I mentioned, the Common Application enables you to apply to 250 colleges with one basic form. (See p. 48.)

✓ **If you prefer and are potentially admissible to colleges with mainly A students, apply to**

five to seven colleges with mainly A students. (These schools are tough to get into, so you need to apply to at least five to increase your chances of getting into at least one.) AND

two to three colleges that you can count on getting into. Choose these probably safe colleges as carefully as the others. You may end up there! One safe college should also be financially safe—a college at which you're confident you'll be admitted and sure your family can comfortably afford.

✓ **If you prefer and are potentially admissible to colleges with some B and some A students, apply to**

three to five colleges with some B and some A students AND

two to three colleges with many B– students that you can count on getting into. Choose these probably safe colleges as carefully as the others. You may end up there! One safe college should also be financially safe—a college at which you are confident you'll be admitted and sure your family can afford.

✓ **If you prefer and are potentially admissible to colleges with many B– to C+ students or two-year colleges, apply to**

three to five of those. Be sure to include one financially safe college—one at which you're confident you'll be admitted and sure your family can afford.

Step 7: College Fairs

Sure, college fairs are convenient because many colleges send representatives there. But remember that you'll be talking with the colleges' salespeople. Even so, they can be somewhat useful if you know what to ask.

Don't ask questions designed to dig up dirt because college reps usually won't cooperate. Questions likely to yield useful information include "What makes your college different than other small (large) rural (urban) colleges?," "What programs is the college particularly proud of?," "What sort of student is such a good fit for your college that you'd tell him it's worth coming across the country to attend?"

Take notes in your college notebook after visiting each college's representative. Otherwise, the colleges may blend together.

Step 8: Make an Actual Visit

You wouldn't marry someone you've never met. Yet many students commit to a college without checking it out in person. Mistake.

Don't worry about appearing out of place. Every year, thousands of high school students can be seen poking around college campuses with their parents asking questions that make their children's faces red.

The main purpose of a visit is to see how you feel among these students. A pretty campus and fancy facilities are nice, but in the end, your happiness will depend more on how well you fit in. And a smart visit can help you judge that. Secondary purpose: if it's a college to which you're unsure you'll be admitted, a visit and on-campus interview may boost your chances. A visit

> **Usually interviews are *not* required. If it's optional, here's a rule of thumb: Interview only if most adults enjoy talking with you.**

shows you're serious about attending, your answer to the essay question "Why this college?" will be more convincing, and if you interview well (see pp. 57–59 for interview tips), it may help a bit more. Usually interviews are *not* required. If it's optional, here's a rule of thumb: Interview only if most adults enjoy talking with you.

INSIDER'S SECRET Many students make a worse decision after a visit than they would have without one. A college can feel so overwhelming that many students come away with little more than, "The campus was beautiful and the tour guide was nice." Too often, luck plays a big role. Did you show up on a rainy day? Get a terrific tour guide?

Here's how to make sure your visit helps you make a wise choice.

WHEN TO VISIT

Consider fall of the senior year; you'll be applying soon so you'll be motivated to take your visit seriously, yet there's still time to add or subtract colleges from your list. Fall is the most popular time to visit, so to be sure you can get an interview and perhaps a dorm stay, make an appointment one to three months in advance, especially if it's a college with mainly A students. An ideal time to visit? Late August or early September, when a college may be in session but your high school is not. But remind yourself of whether that balmy late summer weather will soon yield to a long, bone-chilling winter.

An alternative, especially if you think you might interview poorly, and/or if you're applying to faraway colleges, is to wait until April of your senior year and visit your favorite two or three colleges that admitted you. An April visit means you don't waste trips on colleges that didn't admit you, and your motivation to check them out will be high. And you won't have the fear (a groundless one) that if you ask tough-minded questions, the college will reject you.

When's the worst time to visit? Any time that classes aren't in session: on weekends, and especially during vacations. Visiting then is like test-driving a car with the engine off. Keep in mind that many colleges basically shut down for the weekend. Summer school students are different from the regular ones and the tone of the place changes, so you'll get an inaccurate, yet hard-to-shake, impression. Similarly, don't visit during Spring Carnival or Homecoming. That's not what the campus is usually like. If you're a varsity athlete, consider visiting when your sport is in season.

I have mixed feelings about campus open houses for prospective students. On the upside, there are lots of people around to make you feel welcome and answer your questions. But at open house, there usually is, as Bates College Vice President Bill Hiss says, "a festive atmosphere that is very different from daily campus life."

BEFORE THE VISIT

1. Go with at least one parent. There's a lot to see and four or six eyes can see more than two. Also, it's fun to compare notes. However, when parents hear about the naked parties and keggers, they somehow lose their open-mindedness about that college. So here are some tips:

   ✓ Agree on how much time you and your parent will be separate during your college visit. Many families agree to take the tour together, then separate for a few hours, meet again briefly, then separate again.

✓ Agree that when you're together, it's okay for parents to ask an occasional question but not a nonstop barrage.

✓ Tell your parents if there are things you specifically want them to do or not do. For example, many teens go wild with embarrassment when Mom gives a good-bye kiss.

Just go with friends? Usually fun; only sometimes useful. Some students find it too tempting to goof around.

> **PARENTAL NOTE** Family visits to colleges can be a memorable bonding experience but can also be tough days of concentrated togetherness, especially when such a big decision is at stake: your money, their future. Your child may "hate" you at this age. Meanwhile, you're reminiscing about your good ol' college days, freaking out about your kid leaving, and stressing about having to jeopardize your financial security for the privilege of having a college corrupt your baby. It's a situation ripe for disaster.

2. Plan to visit only one and certainly no more than two colleges per day. If it's a school you're serious about, spend an evening in a dorm.

3. If you're visiting more than one college, try to save your top choice(s) for last. As you go along, you'll learn how to visit and interview more effectively.

4. Call ahead.

✓ Ask whether your selected dates coincide with Homecoming, Parents Weekend, the first week of class, finals week, or other inappropriate times for a visit.

✓ Ask the admissions office if you can spend the night in a dorm, perhaps with a student in your prospective major. (Bring a sleeping bag.) This serves a second purpose: It lets the admissions office know that you're seriously considering this college. It likes admitting students who are likely to show up in September.

✓ Make motel reservations for Mom and Dad (unless you'd like them to sleep in the dorm with you).

✓ If you want an interview, make an appointment. If you have a prospective major, schedule an interview with a professor in that department. Not only will you learn about the department, but if you're impressive (or if the department is hungry for students), the professor may put in a good word for you with the admissions office.

✓ Get travel and parking directions. It feels terrible to arrive clueless and nervous at a strange campus. I've seen families unfairly turned off to a college just because they got off to a bad start. You can get point-to-point directions free online at *www.mapquest.com.* Cross-check that against directions from *maps.yahoo.com/dd.*

✓ If the college's sticker price will strain your family's budget, make an appointment with the financial aid *officer,* not a counselor. Be sure to read Chapter 5 first.

✓ If you're an athlete, musician, or actor, ask the admissions office to give you an appointment with the coach or director.

5. On the way to the college, reread your notes on that school, college guide write-ups on the college, and material the college sent you.

DURING THE VISIT

Beware of tour guides, the time, the weather, and the physical campus. Here's why.

Tour Guides

Tour guides are almost always enthusiastic, unless, of course, they're in a bad mood, neither of which, of course, affects whether you would be happy at this college.

Time

If you happen to visit a college at noon, that's when most colleges are most alive. Students are buzzing around campus amid folks hawking hand-crafted jewelry or urging you to join their clubs or causes, all perhaps accompanied by a rock band. But arrive at 4:30, and even the most dynamic college won't seem as exciting.

Weather

No matter how great the college, rain, not to mention slush, can't help but dampen enthusiasm for it. Think about the *typical* weather at the college, not that day's weather.

The Physical Campus

It's easy to be awed by ivy-covered walls, lush lawns, and chiming bell towers. But for most people, the campus' attractiveness ends up having only a modest impact on their happiness and success. As a student at the lovely University of the South said, "The beauty wears off, so if you don't have a better reason for going to that college, you may be in trouble." Remember, manicured lawns and pristine buildings are ultimately paid for by students. When you realize that your tuition cash is being blown on shrubs, you may not find it so beautiful.

So, as soon as you arrive, say aloud three times:

✓ I won't let the tour guide sway me.

✓ I won't let the day's weather sway me.

✓ I won't let the college's brand name sway me.

✓ I won't let the campus's beauty (or lack thereof) sway me too much. (Don't be like one of my clients, whose family drove six hours to visit a college, took one look, and insisted that her father turn around without ever having left the car. She found the buildings "sterile-looking.")

Be sure to do at least some of the following:

Bring a memo pad.

See something you want to remember about the college? Write it down right then. Otherwise, it's easy to forget, and in a week, colleges start to melt together. Was it Mary Washington College or St. Mary's College of Maryland that had those great instructors? Also, you'll be able to jot down the names, phone numbers, and e-mail addresses of students and professors you met so you can ask follow-up questions or send thank-you notes.

Take pictures.

Take pictures of what you want to remember about the college: the inspirational professor, the student that typifies the place, the dorm that looks like a bomb hit it, the great recreational sports facilities, the chicken tetrachloride. Begin with a picture of something with the college's name on it (for example, the college's main gate), or you'll forget which college goes with which pictures. Think you'll feel like a raging dork with a camera? Remember, the only difference between you and them is that they're enrolled dorks. Besides, if you do enroll, they'll never remember you. All dorks look alike.

Take the tour.

Try to do it early in your visit. It will orient you. But remember that the tour guide is probably giving a spiel crafted by the admissions office.

My favorite question for the tour guide: "On your tours, what do you try to emphasize and deemphasize about the college?" (See pp. 30–32 for other questions.)

Answers to questions that might put the college in a bad light—"How's the crime rate?"—are often scripted. Before you get impressed with the fancy equipment that the tour guide shows you, ask yourself or the guide how often you are likely to be using it. Before you get impressed with the world-class researchers, ask whether they're really good teachers or just good researchers, and how much are you likely to be taught by them. My favorite question for the tour guide: "On your tours, what do you try to emphasize and deemphasize about the college?" (See pp. 30–32 for other questions.)

After the tour.

If your parent is with you, split up for at least part of the time. Divide the detective work, then meet every so often to compare notes and figure out what to do next.

Never leave a college campus without asking questions of at least seven students that the admissions staff did NOT put in front of you. Don't just speak with who's paid by the college, speak with who's paying the college. In addition to getting the straight scoop, you'll feel what it's like to be around this college's students.

Here are some ways to get the real lowdown on college life:

Grab 'em. I know it's scary, but approach friendly looking students at a campus hangout (student union, plaza, dorm recreation room, cafeteria, coffee house) and ask a question or two. Most students love to talk about their school. You might start with something like, "I'm thinking of coming to this college and thought I should talk with some students. What should I know about it that I couldn't find out in the official brochure?"

Eavesdrop. Listen in on a few cafeteria tables' conversation. Do you like these students? Could you imagine yourself in a discussion like that? (Are people talking about issues other than whether *ER* is a good show?) When you feel brave, go over to a group of students, tell them that you're a high school student considering this college, and are trying to learn more about what it's like. They'll probably clue you in on all sorts of stuff and be more open than you'd expect. After all, they were in your shoes not long ago.

More cafeteria clues. While you're in the cafeteria, sample the food. Tasty morsels or mystery meat? If you're vegetarian, is there more than a salad bar and soggy veggies?

Most colleges claim to celebrate diversity. The cafeteria is a great place to assess the reality because, there, integration is voluntary. Do people of different races eat together or do they self-segregate?

Drop by the student newspaper office. Newspaper folk are excellent sources of information about a college. Also, pick up a few copies of the campus newspaper. What stories make the front page? What's in the letters to the editor? What's on the campus calendar of events?

Visit ten classes in half an hour.

Sitting in on one class can be misleading—the professor could be a campus star or a campus joke. Instead, ask someone to point out a building in which a wide range of undergraduate classes is taught, especially those in your prospective major.

INSIDER'S SECRET Stroll down the halls and peek in five to ten doors, or duck in the back row of a large lecture class. (People do it all the time. Some even get grades.) Are most professors interesting or are they the answer to your insomnia problem? Do the students seem involved or are you seeing heads about to crash on desktops? Spend a minute in back of five or ten classes and you'll get the picture. Would you want to attend four years of such classes?

Some students say they're too shy to stand outside a classroom door or duck into the back row of a large class, but it's worth conquering the shyness. Shouldn't you sample a few classes before buying four to six years worth?

Check out the quality of the program in your prospective major.

Ask the secretary in the office of your prospective major to point you to an *advanced* class in that major that will be ending in a few minutes. Head over there and wait for the class to be dismissed. Then stop a group of students and ask a question like, "I'm thinking of coming to this college and majoring in X. What's the major like? Do most graduates get good jobs or into good graduate schools?"

How available are professors?

Walk down a hall of professors' offices. How many are in their offices? How many are meeting with students?

Look at the bulletin boards.

They are windows to the soul of a campus. Which flyers are most common: political action rally, expensive stereos for sale, semi-formal dances?

Check out the facilities.

For example, the on-campus housing, the recreational basketball courts, student center, dining halls, libraries, and so on.

What's near the campus?

Stroll through the blocks next to campus. Lots of bookstores, coffee houses, movie theaters? Affordable stores? Do you feel safe walking the streets? How easy is it to get to the nearest big city?

Visit a dorm in the evening.

I know it's an uncomfortable thought. "I'm a high school kid. I'll feel weird spending an evening with college students." Luckily, it usually ends up being fun as well as informative. A bunch of students will probably cluster around you, dying to reveal the inside joys and the inside dirt. Rats in the dorm? They've been seen even in ritzy colleges' dorms, but you won't learn that in the official brochure. You'll also see what the students are like. Too studious? Too raunchy? Too radical? Too preppy? Is the atmosphere like Animal House, an academic sweatshop, or a good balance? Life can vary a lot from dorm to dorm, so around 10 or 11 P.M. visit a couple of others. As you leave, ask yourself, "Would I be glad to live with such students?"

MASTER LIST OF QUESTIONS TO ASK ABOUT A COLLEGE

It may be safest to ask students, not admissions officers, the most probing of these questions, but don't be intimidated. Many students fear that if they ask a hard question of an admissions representative, they won't be admitted. Sure, if you ask five, you might be perceived as a problem, but ask a tough question or two and, if anything, your chances of being admitted will increase. The college will respect you for being a good consumer.

General Questions

What are some good and bad things about the college?
Do you feel the college is worth the money?
What sorts of students fit best and worst here?
What should I know about the college that wouldn't appear in the
    official brochure?
What legitimate gripes do students have about the college?

Why do students transfer out?

If you could do it again, would you choose this college?

Describe yourself. Then ask what the college is like for people like you. For example, "I'm shy, enjoy discussing intellectual things, and African American. How well would I fit here? What would I have to do to fit well?" Other ways you might characterize yourself: artsy, intellectual, social, religious, liberal, not materialistic, love sports, study five hours a night, a free spirit.

Academics

How good are the professors?

What's the typical class size?

Is it easy to get into the classes you want?

What are some outstanding majors?

Do you get to hear diverse perspectives or mainly just the liberal or just the conservative point of view?

How easy is it to get a professor to take a real interest in you?

Are there many opportunities for students to work one-on-one with faculty: for example, independent studies or working on faculty research?

Are the dorm rooms wired into the campus computer network?

I have a learning disability. What accommodations are made? (Ask this at the disabled student services office.)

Campus Life

What are the best housing options?

How good is the orientation for new students?

What's it like in the dorms?

Does overcrowding ever force the college to cram three students into a dorm room built for two, or even to force students to live in local motels?

Is it quiet enough to study in most dorm rooms?

How many hours a week do most students study?

How's the food?

What's the weather like?

What's it like for minorities (or gays, adult students, etc.)?

Are there many commuting students? Does that make the campus too quiet?

What do most students do on the weekends?

Is there much political activism?

How big a role do alcohol or drugs play in social life?

How big a role do fraternities and sororities play in campus life? If you're not in one, what are your social options?

Do you need a car?

What are big issues on campus?

Is safety an issue? (Also, ask the local police department for the crime statistics on and near campus. Most campus crime occurs near, not on campus.)

Athletes and musicians ask coaches: How much will I get to play? What makes your program different from your competitors'?

Athletes and musicians ask other players: What's the coach (or director) like?

What does the college do to help ensure that graduating students find good jobs?

RIGHT AFTER YOU LEAVE CAMPUS

Complete the College Visit Report Card on p. 34. You may think you'll remember how you feel about the college, but it's safer to write it down immediately.

Consider writing or e-mailing a thank-you note to the admissions staff member who met with you. It can be as simple as this:

Dear X,

Thanks for taking the time to meet with me. I enjoyed our discussion about _____. Thanks for helping me learn more about Utopia College. I'm glad you were impressed that I *[insert something she liked about you].*

Hoping to get a fat envelope,

Sincerely,

Make a Copy of the Following for Each College You'll Visit

MY VISIT TO _____ COLLEGE

(Take this with you on your visit. When it's complete, attach it to the page in your notebook for this college.)

Pre-visit Information

Directions to campus and the interview:

Name(s) of person I am to interview with:

Date and time(s) of interview:

Time of tour:

Name and phone number of student I'll be staying with:

Where and when to find this student:

Questions I want to ask of students:

Questions I want to ask of college representatives:

COLLEGE VISIT REPORT CARD

Academic Life: Excellent   Good   Fair   Poor

Comments:

Campus Life: Excellent   Good   Fair   Poor

Comments:

The Students: Ideal   Good   Fair   Poor

Comments:

Overall Impression: Excellent   Good   Fair   Poor

Comments:

Step 9: Decide Among the Colleges That Admitted You

The best decision is usually one in which you gather lots of information and then go with your gut feeling. In most cases, just reread your notes on the colleges in your college notebook, run your decision by your college counselor, attend one of the online or in-person open houses for admitted students, and compare costs. Be sure to take your financial aid award into account, especially the cash part (pp. 91–92 tells you how to do this).

INSIDER'S SECRET If you're not satisfied with your financial aid award, negotiate or have your parent negotiate with one of the college's financial aid officers. Often, you can get more aid, especially if you provide new information. For example, another college offered you a better deal, your family has big medical or home repair expenses, or a divorce is impending. For more on negotiation, see p. 92.

If, by the May 1 deadline, you haven't received financial aid awards from all the colleges you applied to, ask for an extension from the colleges you're still considering. Usually, it will be granted.

Think twice about getting advice at the last minute. At this stage, you're vulnerable. A single person's comment can outweigh a year of investigation.

If you haven't been admitted anywhere, see pp. 63–64.

When it's actually time to make your final decision, it's tempting to simply choose a brand-name college. For some students, a highly selective college such as an Ivy or Williams is a wise choice—when you know you'll thrive best among top students. Earlier, however, for many students, I've

> **Don't say yes to a college until you've gotten financial aid offers from all colleges that offered to admit you. Aid packages can vary wildly!**

explained why brand-name colleges may be ill-advised, but perhaps another dose of caution might help here at the moment of truth. A study reported in the *American Economic Review* said, "While sending your child to Harvard may appear to be a good investment, sending him to a local state university to major in engineering and take lots of math and preferably attain a high G.P.A. is an even better investment. Apparently, what matters most is not which college you attend, but what you did while you were there…Measured college effects are small, explaining just one to two percent of the variance in earnings."

Loren Pope, author of *Colleges That Change Lives*, writes, "In March, 1994, *The New York Times* reported that a quarter of Harvard's class of 1958 had lost their jobs, were looking for work, or on welfare, just when their careers should have been cresting." The story went on, "Many in the class of '58 thought their degrees ensured career success. They were wrong." The autobiographical sketches written for the 35th reunion "did not radiate with expressions of success and optimism," said author and Yale professor Erich Segal. "Quite the contrary, they seemed like a litany of loss and disillusion." And Harvard was not alone. Alumni groups at other Ivy League schools, the story added, "are reporting

> **Puhleeze, pick your college, not based on brand name, but on the important information this chapter has taught you how to obtain.**

that their members in growing numbers are suffering from the upheavals in corporate America. If there is a lesson in all this it is that a degree from a college like Harvard is no longer the lifetime guarantee of success in careers that it used to be."

Charles Eliot, former president of Harvard University, said, probably only half joking, "It is true that Harvard has become a storehouse of knowledge. The freshmen bring so much and the seniors take away so little."

The title of Harvard graduate and current *Washington Post* education columnist Jay Mathews' 2003 book is apt: *Harvard Schmarvard*.

I frequently pick on Harvard because it's considered the ultimate designer-label college. But the same criticisms could equally be leveled at all the big-name colleges: the other Ivys, Stanford, Northwestern, even the smaller prestige colleges, such as Amherst, Williams, and Oberlin.

PARENTAL NOTE Too often, at this point, all the care in selecting the right colleges can go up in smoke. Johnny decides he wants to go to the college his friends are going to. Janie gets scared she might get lonesome so, at the last minute, she decides to stay close to home. José hears some student rave about College X and suddenly he ignores all his research and decides that College X is the perfect choice. Your job at this point is to be a calming influence. Remind your child of how wisely he had identified his top-choice colleges.

Common Conundrums

Here's how I typically respond to my clients' most frequent concerns about choosing a college. Of course, how I respond depends on the particular student I'm talking with, but I hope these generic responses will help you.

All the colleges seem alike.

They do tend to be quite alike. Most colleges offer similar classes, extracurriculars, and residence halls, and have pretty campuses. Their key differences usually boil down to two things: the student body and the location.

✓ **Student body**. Some colleges have mainly A students, others B students, still others C students. Most colleges have a mix of all types, but other colleges have predominantly artsy, jocky, preppy, activist, and/or studious students.

✓ **Location**. Some colleges are in the tundra; at others, you can wear shorts in February. You also need to decide whether you want to be within laundry distance of home or move to the most far-flung place on the continent.

Unless there's something unusual you're looking for in a college, such as vegan cafeteria food or a major in entomology, chances are, if you choose your college based just on student body and location, you'll be satisfied with your choice.

My girl(boy)friend is going to XXX College.

Romance is a powerful motivator. It can even make a student go to an inappropriate college just to be with Snookums. Of course, if your honeybunch is going to a college that's also well suited to you, okay. But the fact is, most high school romances don't last beyond a semester or two of college—there are too many new people to meet and new experiences that make one of you realize that you weren't so perfect for each other, after all. It would be a shame if you risked your college experience on a relationship that ended soon after you got to college. If your relationship is that perfect, frequent visits, e-mails and big phone bills will keep the relationship thriving even if you attend different colleges.

My parent is pushing College X.

The question is, *why* are they pushing College X? Because it's their alma mater? Because *they* would like to go there? Because they want you close to home to avoid their being lonely? Or because they have a rational reason for thinking it would be a great fit for you? Don't accept nor reject their recommendation without seriously considering their rationale. Perhaps they're right—after all, they probably know you pretty well.

(For parents) I feel guilty about pushing my child toward low-cost colleges.

There really is no reason to feel guilty. The research shows no clear link between college cost and quality. Focus on finding a low-cost college that is well suited to your child. When the college is selected, urge your child to read Chapter 6 in this book on how to make the most of college. Following that chapter's advice will usually do more to enhance your child's college experience than spending money on a pricey college.

I still have no idea where I want to go.

If you've tried to figure out where to apply and still are utterly confused or overwhelmed, this list of my personal favorite colleges can be a useful starting place.

I chose them based on quality of undergraduate education, quality of life, true diversity of ideology encouraged, prestige, and a sticker price that represents good value. (Low-income applicants may get enough financial aid to make the sticker price less important.)

Small Liberal Arts Colleges

Northeast
A students: Amherst or Haverford
B students: Mount Allison (Canada)

Midwest
A students: University of Chicago
B students: Grinnell

South
A students: Davidson
B students: Mary Washington if money is an issue, Rhodes if it is not.

West
A students: Pomona
B students: Santa Clara

Large Colleges

Northeast
A students: Harvard
B students: Penn State

Midwest
A students: Northwestern
B students: Indiana University, Bloomington

South

A students: University of Virginia, Charlottesville; University of North Carolina, Chapel Hill

B students: University of Florida

West

A students: University of California, Los Angeles

B students: University of Washington

Many Studious Students

Northeast

A students: Swarthmore

B students: St. John's (MD)

Midwest

A students: University of Chicago

B students: Carleton

South

A students: Davidson

B students: Rhodes

West

A students: St. John's (NM)

B students: Occidental

Many Unconventional Students

Northeast

A students: Brown

B students: Sarah Lawrence

Midwest

A students: Grinnell

B students: Earlham

South
A students: New College (FL)
B students: Guilford

West
A students: Reed
B students: Evergreen State

The Final Test

Here's a final test of how you feel about the college you've selected. Ask yourself:

Would I be happy living and learning with these types of students
    for four years?
Would I be happy with these professors for four years?
Would I be happy living in this environment for four years?
Will this college really help me achieve my goals?
Is this college worth the money?

If the answer to all five questions is yes, you've found a good new home. Congratulations.

Remember!

1. Ninety-five percent of colleges need you more than you need them—because most colleges never fill all their slots. Be choosy!

2. The best ways to learn about a college:

   ✓ Read about them in one or more of these guides:
      — *The Best 357 Colleges* (Each college's profile summarizes what more than 100 of its students say about their college.)
      — *The Fiske Guide to Colleges*
      — *Barron's Guide to the Most Competitive Colleges*
      — *Barron's Best Buys in Higher Education*

✓ Read some issues of the college newspaper—often available at the college's web site or at *dir.yahoo.com/News_and_Media/College_ and_University/ Newspapers.*

✓ Ask the college to send you a copy of their most recent student satisfaction survey and visiting team accreditation report (my favorite tools for evaluating a college).

✓ When visiting prospective colleges, never leave a campus without talking with at least seven students that the admissions office did not put in front of you.

✓ A good way to assess the quality of teaching at a college is to walk down the halls of a busy classroom building and stop in front of five or ten open doors. Would you like to be in that class?

3. In making your final choice, yes, a brand-name college offers advantages, but lesser-known colleges also have advantages. **Pick the college that is right for you.** Ultimately, you will be happier and more successful.

Getting Into
Killer Colleges Without
Killing Yourself

"Highly qualified students are denied by the hundreds at competitive colleges. Admission officers at Stanford turned away 500 of the 800 valedictorians who applied last year. The Ivys and Nearly Ivys and Georgetown did too. Princeton is the first to admit that it turns away many students who are better than the ones it takes."

Journal of College Admissions

"I am frustrated by the way the selective college admissions process diminishes so many of our children . . .Children needn't be whip-sawed by what is arguably the most successfully marketed product in America."

Bill Mayher, author of
The College Admissions Mystique

Imagine that you wanted to buy a Toyota, but the salesperson said, "I'm sorry, but before we can take your money, you must complete a detailed application so we can determine if you're among the 15 percent who are qualified to own a Toyota." You apply, wait months, and finally receive a fat envelope that says, "Congratulations! You have been selected!" Wouldn't you be even more eager to buy the car? Might you even be willing to pay even more for the privilege of being in such an exclusive club?[1]

---

[1] This metaphor is from Bill Mayher, author of *The College Admissions Mystique*.

The same is true of a college. If it's hard to get into, it seems more desirable. That's ironic because, as explained earlier, less prestigious colleges may be as good or better, even for your career. Plus, less prestigious colleges don't require you to orchestrate your entire high school life just so it looks good on your college application, nor do they require stratospheric SAT scores so you feel forced to make SAT preparation your main extracurricular activity. And most less selective colleges charge much less money.

If you're willing to limit yourself to the 3,850 out of the nation's 4,000 colleges that don't play the hardball admission game, you can probably skip this entire chapter.

INSIDER'S SECRET There's even a back door into many of the 150 tough-to-get-into colleges: Get your degree through their night or extension programs—even Harvard offers one. That's a smart option: easier to get into, less expensive, the same or better professors, midlife as well as younger students to broaden classroom discussions, and the designer label on your diploma. All you miss is the overrated dorm life.

If, however, you insist on the traditional route into the Killer 150, this chapter will show you how to up maximize your chances.

Step 1: Take the Hardest Schedule You Can Without Getting a C in Any Academic Subject.

Sound like fun so far? Alas, the first thing Killer Colleges look for is great grades in tough courses. I wish I could tell you that colleges salivate at Intro to Photography, but the fact is, they look for transcripts with five or more academic subjects per term, most of which are honors, Advanced Placement, or International Baccalaureate classes, especially in the 11th and 12th grades.[2] These colleges value these courses so much that they generally prefer a B in an honors class to an A in a

---

[2] I believe it is not in the developmental best interests of even the most highly capable students to be taking that heavy a load.

regular one, though of course, they really want to see As in honors courses. Nice of them, huh.

Step 2: Don't Dabble. Focus.

Killer Colleges prefer students who have explored one extracurricular activity in depth. So to enhance your admissibility, devote most of your extracurricular effort to just one or two pursuits: whether athletic, artistic, entrepreneurial, or altruistic. High school should be a time to explore. Unfortunately, colleges are more concerned with assembling a student body in which each student is an expert in something, even if that means you have to pick prematurely.

IMPORTANT! Please, do not choose an extracurricular activity to impress the colleges, taking that sport or volunteer position you're dreading just because you think it will up your college admissibility. One girl, on the advice of an expensive college counselor, joined her high school's crew team. This meant she had to wake daily at 4 in the morning, take the bus to the marina where the team practiced, and then at 5, brace for the cold while rowing until she reached her pain threshold. I don't care if it got her into Harvard (it didn't). She made herself miserable for two years in the service of getting into a brand-name college, which might or might not have made her any happier or more successful than the college to which she would have been admitted had she not compromised herself.

Step 3: Decide Whether to Take the SAT or ACT, and Whether You Need to Prepare. If You Need to Study, It's Not Worth Going Overboard.

Almost all colleges will accept either the SAT or ACT, but which should you take?

INSIDER'S SECRET If you're bright but lazy, try the SAT. If you're a plugger, have a learning disability, or are weak in math, consider the ACT. Only 25 percent of the ACT is math, versus 50 percent on the SAT. Another factor: 25 percent of the ACT is science, and there is no science section on the SAT.

Should you prepare? Take a sample SAT or ACT under timed conditions. The actual past SATs are available in a book called *10 Real SATs*. For the ACT, actual past exams are available in the book *Getting into the ACT.*

Don't waste time preparing if your score on the sample test is high enough to be in range for your top-choice colleges (check out *collegeboard.com, review.com,* or *usnews.com*).

How high is high enough? Because of a recent Supreme Court decision (*Gratz* v. *University of Michigan*), it's prudent to adjust your target SAT score by your race. If you are Black, Hispanic, or Native American, your score is probably high enough if your score is at the 25th percentile of the college's admission range. If you are white or Asian, you can have the same level of confidence only if your score is at the 75th percentile. (Of course, your grades and other factors are usually more important determinants of your admissibility.)

IMPORTANT! The racial differences in admissibility may be even more extreme if a pending federal law passes allowing states to offer illegal aliens admission to U.S. colleges plus the right to in-state tuition.

If your score on the sample test is more than 125 SAT points below your target score on the old SAT (200 points on the new SAT) or 5 points on the ACT, consider easier-to-get-into colleges. It's unlikely you'll improve your score enough even if you take an expensive test-prep course.

IMPORTANT! The average improvement is just 28 to 125 points on the old SAT (42 to 187 on the new SAT), or 1 to 5 points on the ACT, depending on which study you believe. And to get that, you'll have to study regularly for the test, which usually takes time from studying for your courses. That can lower your course grades, which is what counts most in college admissibility. Besides, you'd probably find that harder-to-get-into college too difficult anyway.

If, however, your score is 25 to 125 old SAT or 40–200 new SAT points (1 to 5 ACT points) lower than your target, here's a smart, easy, and inexpensive approach to improving your score. This approach will boost your score almost as much as an expensive course, you will do it in lots less time, and you will do it for lots less money. Here's what to do:

✓ To avoid a low math SAT or ACT score, keep taking math. If you're taking precalculus or calculus in your junior year, review your algebra and geometry before taking the test.

✓ Use the free study materials sent to you when you registered.

✓ Get a test-prep guide. Barron's as well as other companies publishes guides for the SAT and ACT in book and CD-ROM formats.

✓ The new SAT includes an essay. Contact your English teacher for advice on how to do well on SAT essays.

When should you take the SAT or ACT?

It's probably best to take the SAT in May or the ACT in June of your junior year. At that time, a full school year of learning will be fresh in your mind. Taking it then also gives you an idea of which colleges to consider, and allows time to retake the test in October, if needed.

Should you retake the test?

Retaking rarely results in a big enough increase to improve your college admissibility. And the study time for the retake often is time taken away from studying for your courses, which can lower your grades, and *that* can reduce your college admissibility. A final reason not to retake: colleges receive all your scores. They may say they count only the highest score, but unless the college doesn't let a human see the scores, most decision makers can't help but be affected by seeing the lower scores among the higher ones.

If you've already taken the old SAT, should you take the new one? Only if you did worse than you felt you could have, are better at Algebra 2 than Algebra 1, or if you get good grades on essays.

Be smart about the SAT II

Most colleges don't require SAT II exams, but many of the 150 Killer Colleges require two or three of them. Check each college's application form to be sure, but you're usually safe if you take Math 1C (or 2C if your PSAT or old SAT is more than 700), plus two SAT IIs of your choice.

INSIDER'S SECRET It's tough to get a high score on the physics or Chinese exam because top students take it. Easier tests: biology (ecology option), U.S. history, and Spanish. Prepare by using the free booklet you get when you sign up, and if needed, a commercially available prep book.

The best time to take SAT IIs is at the end of June of your junior year, except for a course that you completed at the end of your sophomore year, such as biology.

Step 4: Get the College Applications.

Ever more colleges allow you, indeed encourage you, to apply online for admission, financial aid, and housing. Just go to the college's web site. The current version of forms is usually available by August or September of your senior year. If an online application is available, it's usually wise to use it.

If you prefer or the college requires a pencil-and-paper version, download it from the college's site or call the admissions office. Copy the blank form, write your application on the copy, and only when it's perfect, copy it onto the original. The college will be impressed with how meticulous you are.

A time-saving application

You can apply to as many as you like of 250 well-known institutions using one application: the Common Application, available and fileable at *www.commonapp.org*. This saves retyping your basic information for each college and in most cases, allows you to use the same essay for each application.

All 250 institutions have signed statements that students who use the Common Application will not hurt their chances of admission. And my discussions with other counselors, especially in the last few years, suggest this is true. To give yourself an additional measure of safety, use the "additional information" space on the application to write a paragraph explaining why you're interested in that college.

Step 5: Make a List of Deadlines.

Think of how miserable you'd feel if after four years of high school coursework, you got rejected from your first-choice college just because you forgot to have your high school transcript or test scores sent to the college on time. It happens, and the college probably won't care if the dog ate it. HINT: Save yourself the grief. On the form on p. 194, write the deadlines for all your colleges. They're listed on the college's web site and on the Common Application.

Two tempting but risky offers from the colleges

To scoop up the best applicants before other colleges can get them and perhaps offer them a bigger discount, many four-year colleges offer one of two options—Early Decision or Early Action—that allow you to apply early (usually by November 1 of your senior year) and get your answer early: usually by December 15. Both options are risky.

EARLY DECISION

On the upside, not only does Early Decision let you know earlier, but your chances of admission are improved. The edge, however, is modest. Don't be deceived by the statistics that a much higher percentage of early applicants are admitted. A major reason is that the pool of Early Decision applicants is stronger. However, if you are a legacy (child of an alum), the Early Decision advantage will be larger—the college views you or your parent as more likely to become big donors.

The problem is that if a college admits you Early Decision, you must attend that college. Many students change their mind between December and May of their senior year, and if you do, you're stuck unless you find the financial aid award inadequate.

INSIDER'S SECRET The financial aid package *is* more likely to be inadequate than if you apply regular decision, because the college knows it doesn't have to compete against other colleges' financial aid packages.

If you're a late bloomer, Early Decision bears an additional disadvantage. The college will judge you without seeing any of your senior-year grades. A related disadvantage of Early Decision is that it can take away an incentive to study hard during the senior year.

EARLY ACTION

Early Action is also dicey. You don't have to commit to the college until May 1, so you can decide to go elsewhere, but the standards for Early Action admission are usually tougher. Sure, you might get a yes earlier, but do you want to pay the price: a bigger risk of getting rejected? And a bigger risk of getting a bad financial aid package?

Warning: Until recently, you could apply to more than one college Early Action, but some prestigious colleges, in violation of a National Association of College Admissions Counselors "Principle of Good Practice," are insisting that applicants apply Early Action only to that college.

Early Action can, however, be a useful strategy for students with outstanding records through the junior year, who have completed all their SAT/ACT testing by October, and whose grades are likely to be lower in the senior year.

INSIDER'S SECRET Except in the above case, I believe it's generally smarter to apply regular decision. Then in February, write a note to your top-choice colleges explaining that each is a prime contender. Colleges want to offer spots to students who are likely to come. The note can simply say, "I just want to let you know that having learned more about the colleges, yours is now my among my top choices. [Give two or three reasons why.] I'm really hoping you'll admit me."

One great offer . . . for the right student

Bored to tears in high school? Feel mature enough to go to college after your junior year? Here's an "early" option that may make sense: Early *Admission*. Many colleges allow exceptional students to begin college after their junior year of high school. To apply for Early Admission, you must apply by May or June of your junior year, and have taken your SAT or ACT in your junior year.

Step 6: Complete the Applications.

If you're a procrastinator, hang a list of your list of application deadlines on the wall or around your neck. Ask your parents to pester you about them. (Like they won't anyway.) If pestering you doesn't work, could it be a sign that you don't want to go straight to college? Should you consider a time-out year? (See pp. 64–66)

> **PARENTAL NOTE** For most students, applying to colleges can be a logistical challenge. This isn't the best time to allow your child to learn from his mistakes, so, starting in September of the senior year, if you see that your child isn't making good progress on the applications on his own, ask your him or her to post the chart on page 194 on the refrigerator. Every few days, look together at the chart to see how things are progressing.

Better to list the few extracurriculars you've really focused on than a bunch of quickies like one semester in the chess club, one summer of football camp, and one week of ladling soup to the homeless. Killer Colleges, look for "sustained interest and increased success." For example, they're impressed with the student who, as a sophomore, wrote for the student newspaper, as a junior, became managing editor, and as a senior, started an alternative paper.

If you're an athlete, visual or performing artist, or debater, throw in a tape. If you're a writer, send a sample. If you're a computer programmer, send your best creation.

In addition to *the* essay, many colleges require short essays on topics such as, "Why this college?" These are can be almost as important as the long essay. If you decided to apply to a college by following the steps in Chapters 1 and 2, you'll write a great answer to this question.

Colleges often ask an unfair question: "What other colleges are you applying to?" Your admissibility should depend on your qualifications, not how many or which colleges you apply to. Colleges want to offer slots to students likely to say yes, but you shouldn't be penalized for making the extra effort to apply to more schools. So, I recommend you list only two to four colleges.

Do your essay

Are your parents nagging you to start your college essays? They've clearly forgotten the mental paralysis, the "I don't know what to write" syndrome that has afflicted every college-bound student since the Marquis de Sade invented the darn thing.

IMPORTANT! Don't even think about downloading an essay from the Net or getting someone to write your essay. One reason is that you might spend the rest of your life worrying whether the only reason you got into the college is that you plagiarized. If you're motivated more by fear than morality, know that if a college sees that your admission essay is much better than your high school grades and SAT scores would have predicted, they will be suspicious and could downgrade or reject your application.

This eight-step approach works for many essay topics:

1. Think of how you could benefit the college.
   You ask, "How can a teenager benefit a college?" Many ways:

✓ Are you the sort who participates a lot in class? Think of times when you sparked an interesting discussion.

✓ Do you have a personality characteristic that will enhance campus life? Are you enough of a leader to start a skydiving club? Enough of an individualist to start a conservative students club at a liberal school? Compassionate enough to help overwhelmed students? Persistent enough to keep revising your article until it gets published?

✓ Can you excel in an on-campus extracurricular? Could you write an addictive weekly column for the student newspaper? Can you play a mean tuba? Are you compelling enough to get dozens of listeners to call in to your campus radio show? Think of an anecdote from your life that proves it.

✓ Are you unusually well matched to the college? If you're looking for a midsized, highly selective southern college with a great biomedical engineering program and you're applying to Duke, you're a great fit.[3]

✓ Would you love to help a prof on his or her research even if your first project is washing 837 test tubes?

✓ Would you add diversity to the student body? Are you a coal miner's daughter? Did you grow up in a Pakistani village? Were you a gang member?

When in doubt, avoid the following topics. They're used so often, they numb admissions officers: how my visit to another country helped me appreciate another culture, how athletics taught me the importance of hard work or sportsmanship, how being in student government taught me the importance of teamwork and leadership, and how important my family has been to me.

If you're stuck, ask yourself, "What have I done to improve my high school or students' experience there?" Or, "If I had to give incoming high school students a speech titled "What I learned from being a teenager," what would my main points be? Or show this page to friends and families and get their ideas.

2. Pick one to four compelling examples that prove you can provide that benefit.

Show, don't tell. Charlene Liebau, director of admissions at Cal Tech, tells of the successful applicant interested in aerospace research.

---

[3] The benefits to the college are that a well-matched student is less likely to drop out, which would the college's statistics look bad, and would cost it money to recruit another student. Also, a well-matched student is likely to be a happy one, and therefore more likely to become an alumni donor.

He wrote about the rocket he built in his garage. He planned to launch it, much to his parents' and neighbors' consternation and to his friends' delight, but in the planning process, he blew up the garage.

3. Tell each example in one or two paragraphs.

Readers of college essays must try to stay awake through hundreds of oh-so-boring pages, so tell your story vividly and clearly. If you're not a great writer, use simple words and short sentences. The more complicated the writing, the more problems are likely to creep in.

If the essay is sounding artificial, make believe you're writing to your favorite relative. Tone is important. If the it sounds phony, filled with clichés such as, "We must celebrate diversity as we move forward to face our challenges," you're dead.

4. Write an introduction that hooks 'em.

An attention-getting statement or statistic is an impressive opener. Here's an introduction with both: "Recently, I read that 85 percent of all high school seniors have been drunk. I'm not surprised."

5. Write a brief conclusion.

One approach is to project into the future. "I plan to continue saying no to alcohol, but yes to many things. I want to say yes to your excellent American history department. I'd like to say yes to writing for the *Flat Hat*. I'd even like to say yes to lots of parties. But most of all, I want to say yes to becoming part of William and Mary's community: top students living and learning together in a beautiful, historic setting. I hope you'll say yes to my application."

6. Revise, put it aside, then revise again (and perhaps again).

A week can help you see that your explanation wasn't clear or that your joke was corny.

✓ Read it aloud, one sentence at a time. Ask yourself, "How can I make this sentence better?" (Clearer? More powerful? In fewer words? More logical?)

✓ Check it again for spelling or grammatical errors.

✓ Have you conveyed that you're moderately confident but not boastful, growing not grown, enthusiastic not whining, respectful but not desperate?

✓ Don't worry if your essay is not clever—for example, "My life is like a drop of water." Of every ten people who try to be clever or cutesy, nine fail. Use the approach recommended here and you may not hit a home run, but you'll be much more likely to get a single or a double, and that's enough to boost your chances of getting admitted.

7. Get some reviews.

Ask a smart person or two to read it, such as an English teacher, college counselor, or smart relative. Ask if the points in your essay seem important, are clearly explained, and are honest. Does the essay reflect who you are?

8. Make one last revision.

Revise based on your reviewers' feedback. Then, read your masterpiece one last time. If you can say, "This is me!" you're finished. Congratulations.

Recommendations

Check the box on the recommendation form that "waives confidentiality." That allows the recommender to write the recommendation without your ever seeing it. If you don't waive confidentiality, most colleges will suspect the recommendation is overly positive.

Chances are a college will ignore letters of recommendation from heavy hitters such as politicians, unless they know you

> **Choose recommenders who are bright enough to write a persuasive recommendation. Even if a letter says you're terrific, colleges won't value it much if it sounds unintelligent.**

well. Alumni who have donated big bucks to the college, however, will likely not be ignored.

A recommender can often support a contention you make in your application. If you say you want to be a history major, you'll probably want a history teacher as a recommender. If your essay describes family problems you've overcome, your counselor might write a letter.

What makes a recommendation persuasive? Specific examples. How do you get your recommender to include specific examples? Just say, "I'm hoping you might mention X" (for example, "that term paper on antiaging drugs in which I interviewed three scientists"). Also, when giving the form to the recommender, offer your resume or list of accomplishments.

Your letter of recommendation may not be at the top of your teacher or counselor's to-do list. Unless your school has told you differently, give your recommenders a stamped envelope with the college's address on it, and in the lower left-hand corner, write, "Deadline for mailing: [insert date]." A few days before the deadline, check back to be sure it will be mailed in time.

Step 7: Bleed Blue and Gold (or Whatever the College's Colors Are).

Many selective colleges have recently added more hoops to jump through if you want to maximize your chances of admission. These colleges track how much interest you've shown in the college: Have you visited the campus? Have you contacted the admissions office with questions? Did you visit that college's booth when the college's rep showed up at your high school?

I oppose this piling yet another set of burdens on the already overburdened students. For example, many students, to avoid unnecessary travel expense and time off school, defer visiting colleges until they find out which colleges admitted them. Now, that prudent action could cost them their admission. Other students are calling all umpteen colleges to which they're applying with a question to demonstrate their serious interest.

When more students wise up to these strategies, all that will have been accomplished is that students will be yet more overburdened, and admissions offices will be even more swamped with questions and visits yet get no more enrollees.

Step 8: Interviewing.

Most colleges don't require an interview, and if required, it rarely sways an admission decision—it's used more to sell you than to judge you. But you can't be sure, so before scheduling an interview, ask if it will be *informational* or *evaluative*.

If it's evaluative, what will you be judged on? Basically, they want to know if you're smart, nice, motivated, and have good values. If most adults like you, you're probably safe. If not, consider not interviewing unless it's required. These tips will help:

✓ Prepare by thinking of a couple of topics you want to talk about, such as a powerful experience or a passionate interest.

✓ Have an answer ready for "Why this college?"

✓ Be prepared to discuss a favorite book.

✓ If there's a reason why you'll be a better college student than your high school transcript or test scores suggest, plan to mention it.

✓ No need for a jacket and tie, but dress well enough to show you care: Guys, wear socks; girls, no bare midriffs.

IMPORTANT! Realize that the interview is a conversation in which you get to ask questions, too. It helps if you go in with a few prepared questions to ask the interviewer, especially ones that will help you decide whether the college is for you, such as, "What about the college are you most proud of?" Don't be afraid to ask a probing question such as, "What's a legitimate gripe that students have about the college?" The interviewer will respect you for being a good consumer. Worst questions: those that are answered on the college's web site.

✓ Don't save all of your questions for the end of the interview. Questions are mid-interview lifesavers. If you've just given a stupid answer to an incredibly easy question and are dying to change the topic, try asking one of your questions. (See pp. 30–32 for my favorites.)

✓ Bring your transcript, especially if you'd like to try to explain away weaknesses.

INSIDER'S SECRET The more highly placed the interviewer, the more an interview can benefit you. So, especially if you think you'll interview well, ask to be interviewed by an admissions *officer* rather than with an admissions counselor or an alum.

Making a Good Impression

Studies have found that you make an extremely hard-to-change impression in the first few seconds you meet someone. How to make a good first impression? It's a sad commentary on human judgment, but all you have to do is follow the advice offered by Gary Ripple, author of *Campus Pursuit*: smile, offer a firm handshake, look the person in the eye, and pleasantly say, "Hi, I'm Rob Jones and these are my parents, Joe and Judy. When should they come back to meet me?" Wait to be invited to sit down, then lean slightly forward, keep a pleasant look on your face (that's pleasant, not psychotic), and maintain eye contact. Believe it or not, in just those few seconds, you're halfway home.

Remember this rule: short answers to hard questions, longer answers to easy ones. That way, more of the interview will be spent on your strengths, which will leave a better overall impression.

The preparation suggested above in the previous paragraphs should ensure the other half.

End by using a similar approach. Smile, look the interviewer in the eye, shake his or her hand, and, if true, say that you enjoyed the interview. If not, thank the interviewer for meeting you.

During the actual interview, be your best self, but be yourself. Interviewers have built-in hogwash detectors.

Frequent mistake: talking too long. You have a green light during the first 30 seconds, a yellow light during the next 30, and a red light after that. If what you said in that first minute was so interesting, the interviewer can ask you more about it. Chances are, he won't.

Another frequent mistake: giving a long answer to a hard question to try to come up with something good to say. Remember: short answers to hard questions, longer answers to easy ones.

Under-the-radar ways to get into killer colleges

1. Choose an unpopular major: philosophy, yes; psychology, no.

2. If you are politically liberal, write compellingly about that in your admission essay. (Be more cautious if you're conservative.)

3. Search the college's web site to find the professor whose work is most interesting to you. Read one of her writings, then phone the professor with questions about it. Ask if she thinks you should consider attending the college. If she says yes, ask if she has any advice for maximizing your chances of admission. In addition to any insider advice, she may volunteer to write a letter on your behalf.

4. Create something: start a club, a business, an alternative newspaper, a nonprofit. You can do it! You'll grow from doing it, and it will impress colleges.

Tips for Athletes and Performers

Ask your coach or teacher if and where you can perform in college. Could you sing for the Yale Whiffenpoofs? For an average college? Or should you confine your singing to the shower? Request, if available, a special coded application for potential varsity athletes.

INSIDER'S SECRET Find teams more likely to need you. Here's how. Visit the web sites of colleges you're considering and look at the team roster. Lots of seniors? They're more likely to need you. Is the college's team just starting up? You're more likely to make the team. This is especially a boon for females—the number of women's teams has almost doubled in the past 20 years.

With your application, include a short note to the college coach or artistic director that includes your performance and academic highlights, and a brief video of you in action. Artists should send slides. Musicians should send a tape. The admissions office will send these materials to the appropriate person for evaluation.

Get on a college coach's "I want" list, and according to James Shulman and William Bowen's book, *The Game of Life*, your chances of admission increase as much as 50 percent, even at the most selective institutions. So, right *after* you've applied to the college (an NCAA regulation), ask your coach to phone or write to colleges on your behalf. For complete advice, go to *www.ncaa.org/eligibility/cbsa*.

IMPORTANT! Potential college varsity athletes must follow a special timeline and regulations. See your coach.

Beware if a coach says, "You're in." Get it in writing. Too often, hyperenthusiastic coaches claim to have more power than they have. Coaches can ask the admissions committee to admit a student but rarely can order it to do so.

Are You a Homeschooler?

The good news is that even prestigious colleges welcome applications from homeschooled students. The bad news is that because you don't have a standard transcript, you usually must prove that your education was at least as good as a typical high schooler's. And yes, that includes science and math.

So, as early as possible, call the colleges on your list to find out what you'll need to do to impress them. At minimum, you'll probably have to take the General Educational Development (GED) exam. In some states, unless you get a waiver from a school district superintendent, this isn't possible until you're 18 or your high school class graduates; ask your prospective colleges how to handle this. You may also need to take three to five SAT IIs. You'll certainly have to meet your state's high school graduation requirements. If you don't know what they are, contact a counselor at a local public high school or a local homeschooling organization.

Whether required or not, submit a log of all your junior year's educational experiences. Include work samples such as essays and reports of science experiments.

You'll also find these resources helpful: *And What About College?* by Cafi Cohen, *Home Education* magazine (*www.home-ed-magazine.com*), and the Home Schooling Legal Defense Association web site (go to *www.hslda.org* and click on "colleges and universities").

If You're Learning Disabled

Mention any learning disabilities on your application. It will probably increase your admissibility at colleges with good support for the disabled, and decrease it at schools with minimal support. If you need the help, you don't want to go to low-support colleges anyway.

For more advice, see Marybeth Kravets's and Imy Wax's *K&W Guide to Colleges for the Learning Disabled.*

If You're Wait-Listed at Your First-Choice College

If you're convinced you'd be much happier at a college that wait-listed you, do the following:

1. **Send a deposit** to a college at which you were admitted. That way you know you have somewhere to go in September.

2. **Call or have your counselor call the college** to find out why Choice 1 failed to recognize your awesome potential. If you need

> You'll probably be as successful at your last-choice college as at your first. Your success will depend far more on what you do than on where you do it.

financial aid, be sure to find out if there's ample financial aid for wait-listed students who later get admitted. (Don't count on it.) Be sure all your financial aid information has been filed with that college.

3. **E-mail or overnight-mail a letter** that expresses your disappointment at being wait-listed. (You needn't tell them you've been sobbing for days.) Give specific reasons why this college is such a good fit, and tell them you will definitely come if you're admitted and receive the needed amount of financial aid (if needed.)

INSIDER'S SECRET To justify a new decision, provide new information, such as your new and improved grades, most-likely-to-succeed award, or even that you kept your grades up—something not all second-semester seniors can claim. Also try to counter the college's objection to you. If the college turned you down because of a weak essay, include another. If it was a low math SAT, include a letter of recommendation from a math teacher. If they thought your extracurricular activities were lame, check that you've described them as well as you can.

4. **Consider a personal appearance** (pronounced "plea"). If you're absolutely dying to go to this college, try one or more of the following

   ✓ If true, say that you are flexible with regard to major, and that if an opening is available in a related area, you would accept that.

   ✓ Ask if you can enroll on a "nonmatriculated basis" (as an unofficial student) and if you get good grades the first term, become officially enrolled next term.

   ✓ Ask if you could be admitted for the spring or summer term. There's often more room then.

   ✓ Ask if you could enroll at a branch campus for the first term, and if your grades are good, transfer to the main campus in the spring.

Pat Ordovensky, author of *Getting into College*, advises that if within two weeks of being wait-listed you don't get a strong indication that you will eventually be accepted, you're better off forgetting your first-choice college. The fact is, the vast majority of applicants on wait lists never get off.

An Editorial

One of colleges' many unfair-to-students practices is their use of the wait list. Many colleges put hundreds of students on the wait list, most of whom never get admitted. For example, in 2003, Williams wait-listed 700 to 800 and admitted 37, and Lehigh wait-listed 2,160 and admitted just 20. Each year, Harvard wait-lists 700 to 1,000 students and, in most years, admits zero to 20.

Why do colleges keep so many students' hopes up in vain? For reasons that make life more convenient for the college.

Some colleges do a lousy job of predicting how many and what kinds of students will show up in September, so they cover their incompetence by putting lots of students on the wait list. If they admit hundreds too few students, no problem. Just go to the wait list. If they guessed right, so what if hundreds of students' hopes are dashed?

Sometimes, there's a more insidious reason. Colleges know that students on the wait list are often desperate to get in—we all want what we can't have. Some foolish wait-listed students agree to forgo financial aid to get admitted. That's music to many colleges' ears: better to have a wait-listed student willing to pay full fare than an admitted student who wants financial aid. Some counselors wonder if colleges deliberately admit fewer students than they need and put the rest on the wait list, knowing that some will come begging: "Oh, please accept me off the wait list. I'll give up financial aid, I'll take a less desirable major; I'll give up my first-choice residence hall. Oh, just please take me!"

A final reason colleges use a wait list: Rather than rejecting a weak student who is the child of a donor or bigwig, or is a minority, some colleges give a courtesy wait-listing to allow the student and family to save face.

If all the colleges have somehow overlooked your wonderfulness

Even if they all turned you down, you still have options.

INSIDER'S SECRET Each May, the National Association for College Admission Counseling issues a list of hundreds of four-year colleges that still need students for the fall term. Many colleges will take a student as late as the second week of class! So will most two-year colleges, which, as I've been stressing, can be smart choices, even for strong students. The NACAC list of colleges accepting late-admission applications is available from May through the summer at *www.nacac.com*.

Senioritis

If, in your senior year, you're fighting with your parents more than Moammar the Mauler fights with Ivan the Hulk, or find that you're doing less homework than you did in the first grade, you may have senioritis. Sure, it can be caused by thinking the second half of the senior year doesn't count,[4] but it may be that you're unconsciously distancing yourself from your high school and family life so you can feel better about going off to college.

There's no easy cure for senioritis. A corny but decent solution is to keep sharing thoughts and feelings with your parents, and try to compromise. There's only one thing I hope you don't make your parents compromise about. If you're doing something that's hurting you (like alcohol or drug abuse), consider letting your parents do what's needed to stop it.

Time Out

Sick of school? Many college students look back and think they wasted their freshman year. Twenty-five percent of freshmen don't return for their sophomore year. To help ensure your freshman year isn't a waste, consider an **interim** semester or year.

If you ask your first-choice college to defer your admission for a semester or year, they'll probably say yes as long as you have something worthwhile planned. Each year, 50 or more students admitted to Harvard defer their admission.

Or if you were turned down by your top-choice schools, an interim year can often change their mind about you.

---

[4]Wrong. An offer of admission can be withdrawn if grades drop significantly. And most Canadian universities make their decision *after* the 12th grade. Besides, the main reason you're in school is not to get grades, it's to learn so you can have a better life. You may not believe me, but I swear it's true.

> **PARENTAL NOTE** I know you're worried that if your child takes time out, he or she won't go to college. The fact is, as long as the interim semester/year is well planned (see below), the odds are excellent that your child will not only go to college but get more out of it. Especially if you think your child is at risk of blowing off the first year of college, encourage an interim semester or year.

First, there are do-it-yourself interim programs. One of my clients simply got a Eurorail Pass, and a copy of *Let's Go*, and explored Europe for a few months, keeping a journal of what prisons were like in each country. Another shadowed a physician for one week, a journalist for the second week, an architect for the third, and an urban planner for the fourth. She liked the physician's week best, but decided that rather than helping people using existing treatments, she'd rather develop new ones. So, she talked her way into a gofer job at a local biotech company. That strengthened her interest in medical research, so she applied to colleges with good molecular biology programs, and was accepted at a more prestigious college than she could have hoped for before her interim year.

A student who enjoys helping people might spend an interim year teaching an illiterate adult to read, as a Big Brother or Sister to a needy child, as a caretaker for a homebound elderly person, or all of the above. Most major cities have a volunteer bureau that can help you find opportunities that would interest you.

Then there are the structured interim programs. Interim specialist Neil Bull suggests a few favorites from among the 2,000 in his database.

> *Environmentalists can work in the Student Conservation Association, which places students in outdoor volunteer programs across the United States. Students interested in health care can try the Frontier Nursing Service, which provides a chance to help people in rural Kentucky. Those looking for overseas experiences can explore the International Internship Network. Whether you are interested in art, finance, or wine making, you can be placed in Spain, Israel, Germany, France, or Italy. Students seeking a more traditional academic year in a foreign culture can choose from among many boarding schools throughout England, India, and Australia.*

For typical students, two to four of these placements constitute the interim year.

An example: Lex Leeming was admitted to Tufts University but felt burned out from school and knew that if he went to college, he wouldn't do well. It was a perfect time to get away without losing any ground. So, Leeming spent a year far from conventional classrooms—building a log cabin on a ranch in Wyoming, helping a documentary filmmaker in upstate New York, serving an apprenticeship in a dive shop in Micronesia, and working as a gardener on the Italian island of Elba. "When I came back, I was totally psyched for my studies," said Leeming, now a sophomore at Tufts. "The year recharged my batteries, my motivation for college, my desire for work. I was excited about life."

Another option is AmeriCorps (*www.americorps.org*), a sort of domestic Peace Corps You'll work on service projects with other young adults, and receive a stipend for your efforts.

You can check out thousands of time-out options using books such as *Taking Time Off, The Uncollege Alternative, The Backdoor Guide to Short-term Job Adventures*, and *The 500 Best Ways for Teens to Spend the Summer.*

Or consider services that put together a custom time-out year for you. For info, go to *www.leapnow.org, www.whereyouheaded.com,* and *www.interimprograms.com.*

Worried that if you take a year off, you won't go to college? Sausalito, California, time-out specialist David Denman says that among the hundreds of students he's worked with, only two haven't gone on to college.

The New York Times reported on a survey of hundreds of graduates of Phillips Academy (a prestigious private high school in Andover, Massachusetts) who had taken an interim year between high school and college. All the respondents said that if they had to do it over again, they would take an interim year.

Beware: An interim year in which you simply sleep late, watch soap operas, slice sausage at the pizza shop, and party doesn't count. The odds of you having a rewarding year—let alone ending up back in college—are small.

For more on helping you decide whether to take time out, see pages 217–219.

Common Conundrums

Here's how I typically respond to my clients' most frequent concerns about getting into college. Of course, how I respond depends on the particular student, but these generic responses may be helpful.

1. **I'm driving myself crazy. I have a test tomorrow, and I'm scared. If I do badly, my course grade will be bad. If my course grade is bad, I may not get into a prestigious college. If I don't get into a prestigious college, I'll have a hard time getting a good job. Noooooh!!!!!!!!!!!**

   There are two other ways of thinking, both valid, that can help keep you calm.

   ✓ *Ambitious But Under-Control Amy*: "I have a test tomorrow. I've been studying all along, but I'm going to allow three hours tonight for studying. If I've put the time in and I still do badly on the test, I'll survive. If I keep putting the time in, I'll get mostly good grades, which is enough to get into one of my top-choice colleges. And about having a good career? That will depend more on how aggressively I look for a job."

   ✓ *Balanced Bob*: "I have a test tomorrow. I figure it's worth about an hour's studying. Then I'll get together with my girlfriend. I'd rather get Bs and have a balanced life than get As and have no life. I know plenty of people who get good educations and good jobs who didn't go to a fancy college."

   Would you rather adopt Amy's mind-set or Bob's? Both are valid.

   Here are the stress management principles embedded in the above:

   ✓ *Concern yourself only with what you can control.* For example, decide how much you want to study, do it, and then let go of the outcome. At that point, there's nothing more you can do about it.

✓ *Consider the long-term effects.* How will one bad course grade affect your life? Will it have much effect on your happiness? Your success? It rarely does.

✓ *Live in the moment.* Spending time regretting the past or worrying about the future ensures you don't enjoy the pleasures of the present—even if it's just the pleasure of listening to what a teacher has to say, what's in that book you're reading, even the taste of the high school cafeteria's tuna sandwich.

2. **Stop being so self-absorbed.** Self-absorbed people spend so much time worrying whether they'll get a B or an A, whether someone likes them, or that they're five pounds overweight. You'll be happier, more popular, and less stressed if you focus on getting things done and helping other people. When you're starting to get preoccupied with yourself, call someone—maybe one of the unpopular kids—ask how they are, and really listen.

3. **School is boring.**

We all feel that way sometimes. The fact is, it's hard for many students to stay excited about quadratic equations, the Peloponnesian Wars, and the halide series of chemical elements. But if you feel bored in school most of the time, you should do something about it. Let me ask you a few questions that can help you figure out what to do:

— Did you feel so bored last year? If not, what's different this year?
— Are you bored in all your classes?
— Sometimes, when we say school is boring, we mean it's too hard or too easy. Are there any subjects you find too hard or too easy? If too hard, should you study harder? Ask more questions of the teacher? Get a tutor? Drop the course? If you find one or more classes too easy, should you tell the teacher and ask for extra-credit work? Ask to be transferred to a higher-level class?
— Would you be more motivated if your parents offered you rewards for good grades?
— Would you be more motivated if you had more friends who were studious?

But what if the problem is simply that you're wondering, "Why do I need to know this stuff?" The fact is, you won't *need* to know most of it, but you'll probably be glad you do. It feels good to go through life knowing the things you learn in high school and college. Also, it enables you to sound like a mature adult when talking with an educated person—perhaps your boss or that cutie you're trying to impress.

4. I did terribly on the SAT (or ACT).

That can feel painful. It's easy to define ourselves by a number, but nothing could be further from the truth. We are all so much more than our SAT score. We are the total of our learning ability, social ability, integrity, quirkiness, hobbies, appearance, and so on. Not only does your SAT score not define you, but it doesn't at all preclude you from ending up at a college at which you'll be happy and successful. Sure, a high score increases your admissibility to hard-to-get-into colleges, but not by as much as you may think. And more important, plenty of good colleges accept students with low SAT scores. If you think your low score was the result of panic or another onetime screw-up, retake the test. Otherwise, turn your attention to more important things.

5. I don't want to take those hard classes.

I can understand that. It's scary to know you may work really hard and still get low grades. And even if you get good grades, it'll just mean you'll get into a more challenging college, which means you'll have to kill yourself even more to get good grades. Indeed, some successful people didn't take really hard courses—they opted for a lighter load so they could enjoy school and life more. So, I'll support you if you decide to lighten your load. But I'm wondering if answering these questions might help you make a more fully informed decision:

✓ Do you think you'd learn more or less in the easier classes?

✓ If you took the easier classes, what would you do with the extra time? Would that be a better use of your time?

✓ Tutors can often help. Do you think that if you had a tutor, maybe just a smart, patient classmate, it would help enough?

✓ Do you think this decision to not stretch yourself is likely to become a pattern? If it is a pattern, you're less likely to be above average in your career. Is that okay with you?

✓ Some people prefer to challenge themselves, even if it means getting a lower grade. How about you?

6. I try, but I still get Cs. I'm a loser.

Believe me, the world won't end if the best you can do are Cs. Plenty of good colleges accept C students. And plenty of C students have gone on to very successful lives: David Letterman and Colin Powell come to mind. But first, let's be sure you've done what you reasonably could to turn at least some of those Cs into Bs:

✓ Are you sitting in the front of the class, so it's easier to pay attention?

✓ Are you asking the teacher for help when you don't understand?

✓ Should you get a tutor, perhaps a student in your class?

✓ Should you take an easier version of a class—for example, a regular class instead of honors?

✓ Should you ask your counselor if you should switch classes to a teacher who is better at explaining things?

✓ Are you spending a reasonable amount of time studying for tests?

✓ Are you reading the textbook each night, not just before the test?

✓ Should you have a study buddy?

✓ Are drugs or alcohol affecting your grades?

7. Stop pushing me: I just want to kick back this summer.

The summer is an awfully long time to be kicking back full time. A carefully selected summer activity or two can help you grow while providing fodder for your college essay. I'm not suggesting you go to summer school, even if it's at a prestigious college. You had plenty of academics last school year and you'll have plenty more coming up. Summer is a good time for a nonacademic experience: learn how to mountaineer, volunteer in a health clinic, take a photography course, whatever.

8. My parents won't stop nagging me to do my college applications.

I know you're under pressure: grades, tests, social life. The last thing you need is your parents nagging you about your applications. You're well aware they're due.

You might find it helpful to put yourself in your parents' shoes. Imagine that you're going to be spending big bucks on your child's college education, and that because of your child's laziness, you might end up having to spend all that money on his or her last-choice college. If your child were taking a too-laid-back approach to applying for college, wouldn't you feel stressed?

Are you taking a too-laid-back approach to those applications? Perhaps your parents, having themselves applied to college, know the process will take longer than you anticipate. For example, it can take quite a while to write and revise your way into a great college essay.

Some students procrastinate so they're forced to do a last-minute job on their applications. Why would they do that? Because, unconsciously, they really don't want to go those colleges, or because, if they don't get in, they can blame it on their laziness: "I could have gotten in if I had tried." Or they need an adrenaline rush to motivate them to do it—even though they know they'll write a bad essay under such time pressure. Does any of that sound like it's what's going on with you?

One way you may be able to get your parents off your back is to make a deal. Say, "I understand you're worried, but I'm feeling too much pressure. How about we agree that I'll get it done by X date *if* you agree not to hound me between now and then?"

If you don't get your essay done by your own deadline, it's a sign you need their nagging or that you need to redouble your efforts to conquer your tendency to procrastinate.

9. **Other kids cheat and download term papers from the Net. They get great grades and it messes up the curve for everyone. If I cheated, my class rank would be so much higher!**

You're right, but you'd be a loser. You may or may not get caught, but it's sure that as you get older, you will cheat more, not less, because you'll grow more dependent on it. That will lower your self-esteem. You may feel that if it weren't for cheating, you wouldn't have gotten as far as you have. You may feel like an imposter. And you'll have learned less, so you will likely fail more in life because many times you simply can't cheat—for example, when presenting at a business meeting. And finally, when you're old and looking back on your life, you may not feel good about the person you were. There are few sadder feelings than feeling bad about how you lived your life. In the long run, the better grades you'll get from cheating will not compensate. I swear.

So, consider getting into the habit of being honest. When you walk into an exam, find a seat far away from anyone. Eliminate the possibility of cheating and you'll derive a side benefit: it will be easier to concentrate.

Every time you're writing a paper, remind yourself that your grade won't go down if you give credit to the author of a quote. It's so easy. If you want to use someone's ideas, fine. Just write, "As Joe Smith said. . . ." I have quoted many people in this book. Do you think less of me?

If you're thinking about letting someone else write a paper for you, remember that if they're writing it, they'll become a better writer and thinker and you won't. In the long run, you'll be the loser.

> **PARENTAL NOTE** One reason students cheat is to meet parental expectations. Make it perfectly clear that you'd rather see an honest C than a cheating A. And if you're not sure that's right, please read the previous section.

Remember!

1. You may not need to study for the SAT or ACT, let alone take a prep course. Take a sample ACT and SAT from a commercially available book that contains past actual exams. Compare your score against the range of scores for students admitted to your top-choice colleges. (You can find that information at collegeboard.com by clicking on "Find a College.") If your SAT and ACT score is in range, just walk in and take that test. If, to get in range, you need to increase your score up to 125 points on the old SAT, 200 points on the new SAT, or 5 points on the ACT, study using the customized self-study program the Inside the SAT/ACT software will generate for you. No need to waste big bucks on a prep course. If you need more than a 125-point old SAT, 200-point new SAT, or 5-point ACT increase to get in range, consider easier-to-get into colleges.

2. Enter your college application deadlines on the form on page 194.

3. For many essay questions, a wise approach is to describe one or more incidents in your life that prove you'd be a valuable addition to a college's community.

4. Just before an admission interview, review the college's web site and its profile in *The Best 357 Colleges, Fiske Guide to Colleges, Barron's Best Buys,* or *Barron's Guide to the Most Competitive Colleges.* Ask the interviewer one or two questions about the college that aren't answered on its web site or in the college guide.

5. Apply to a college Early Decision only if you're sure that college will remain your number one choice and you're willing to risk getting a bad financial aid package.

5

Finding the Money

Students are happy when classes are cancelled.
That makes college the only purchase that people
are happy with when they don't get what they paid for...

Newt Gingrich

$12 billion: *The increase in Harvard's endowment from 1993 to 2003*
66 percent: *The percentage increase in Harvard's tuition from 1993*
                to 2003
$32.5 million: *The profit Harvard makes each year from MBA*
                application fees alone.

Twenty dollars an hour. I'll bet you wouldn't mind making that. But
$20 an hour is nothing compared with what this chapter will probably
earn you. The hour you're about to spend will likely net you thousands
of dollars.

Your parents will probably be paying much of your college expenses,
and much of the advice is aimed at them, so get at least one parent to
read this chapter.

What Does College Really Cost?

Go to many colleges' web sites, and you'll have a hard time finding
out what it costs to attend. Colleges bury that information, because at
brand-name privates especially, the sticker price is frightening to all but
the wealthy. Worse, most colleges underrepresent the actual cost of
attendance. For example, they provide a "cost-of-living" allowance that
is often just half of what the average student spends on clothes, a computer, socializing, trips back home, and so forth. More important, the
number students and parents need for planning purposes is not the one-
year cost, but the cost of obtaining a bachelor's degree. You might ask,

"Then don't we simply need to multiply the one-year cost by four?" No. For decades, most colleges have increased their tuition and fees by much more than inflation. And importantly, *most* students take longer than four years to graduate. According to the National Center for Education Statistics, only 37 percent of bachelor's degree seekers graduate in four years. Many take five or six years, and, of course, many more never graduate.

So, what's the true full cost of getting a bachelor's degree? Let's be optimistic and assume you'll defy the odds and graduate in four years. Let's further assume that colleges will increase their annual tuition only 3 percent

A conservatively derived sticker price of a bachelor's degree obtained in four years at a brand-name public college (in state) averages $90,000; at a brand-name private college $180,000. (Costs at most southern and midwestern colleges are lower.)

rather than the 5 to 10 percent increases that have been more typical. And let's assume your annual living expenses apart from room and board are $7,000 a year—the true average that students spend.

Not surprisingly, many families seriously underestimate the amount of money they'll need to pay for college. Therefore, many students unwittingly apply to unaffordable colleges, and somewhere during the student's education, their parents are forced to inform their child that they can't afford to pay for it.

But, you might ask, what about financial aid? If a college is very desirous of a student, it may offer a generous discount, but the average family earning $70,000 with $50,000 in savings and zero assets in the child's name will likely get NO need-based financial aid at the average brand-name public college. The average family earning more than $130,000 will get little or no need-based cash aid at any college. A family earning lower than those figures will, on average get "aid" that consists heavily of loans. Today, the average financial aid package contains just 39 percent grant money.

The Most Potent Strategy

The easiest if most obvious way to make college affordable is to choose a college with a low sticker price.

Many public colleges are inexpensive, not because they're worse, but because they're subsidized by your parents' tax dollars. You can practically ensure you'll attend a high-quality college if you follow the advice in Chapter 3 on how to pick a college.

And regarding career prospects, if graduates of expensive colleges, on average, get better jobs, it's mainly because those colleges attract better students to begin with. The Harvard name on a diploma is a big plus, but Harvard-caliber students at State U will probably get counterbalancing advantages: great grades without having to

> **You might ask, "At a less expensive college, won't I get a lesser education or have worse career prospects?" The fact is, a college education is one of the few products where higher cost doesn't necessarily mean better quality.**

kill themselves, knock-'em-dead recommendations, strong job leads from impressed professors, and more likely to graduate with decent self-esteem. It is tough to graduate from a college filled with the nation's top 0.0001 percent of driven and/or brilliant students emotionally healthy and with your self-esteem intact. Autobiographies of Harvard alumni 35 years after graduation speak to this.

INSIDER'S SECRET   A study reported in the *Atlantic Monthly*'s College Guide (November 2003) found that the lifetime earnings of students admitted to Ivys who attended less selective colleges was the same as for those who attended an Ivy. Although it's contraintuitive, Harvard versus State U. is probably a toss-up.

The previous paragraph presumes that you're getting into Harvard. The case for a low-cost public college versus a private college is even stronger if we're talking about the many private colleges that are far less prestigious yet cost almost as much as Harvard.

Why graduate costing your family so much money and taking on so much debt? Your savings could buy a wedding, a down payment on a house, or more education. Indeed, with more and more students deciding to go to graduate school, your parents may have to count on paying for college *and* graduate school for each child in your family. Send just two kids to a brand-name public college for a bachelor's and master's degree, and we're talking a quarter of a million dollars! At a brand-name private college, a half million!

INSIDER'S SECRET Some students say they feel guilty making their parents spend all that money. Perhaps they're right. Studies do not find a link between a college's price and its quality. However, for a particular student, it may be worth spending more. If the colleges generated by the College Finder on pp. 6–9 aren't inexpensive, apply anyway. It may be worth the money, especially if you happen to get a generous package—most likely if you're among the top 25 percent of students who enroll at that college. Also apply to a *financial safety school*—one that appears to be a bargain *and* fits you. After you've received the financial aid offers from the colleges, estimate the actual cost of that bachelor's degree, then have an open, honest family discussion about which college is the wisest use of your family's money.

Private College Traps

✓ Most private colleges but only a few public ones, will reduce your financial aid if they they determine that your parents can afford to take an additional mortgage to pay for college.

✓ Most brand-name private colleges but only a few public ones will expect your divorced parent to pay, even if you don't live with him or her.

✓ Some colleges even expect parents who have saved well to use money they were planning on for retirement.

✓ In fairness to private colleges, a few fine ones such as those listed in the first item below, are inexpensive because they're unusually well endowed (wealthy) and can afford to keep tuition low. Most other wealthy private colleges, however, such as the Ivys and Stanford, despite their huge endowments, set their published price such that the true overall cost of a bachelor's degree, even if completed in four years, is around $180,000. However, colleges with strong endowments are more likely to offer a good financial aid package.

Top Values in Higher Education

Low-cost sticker-priced private colleges: Berea, Cooper Union, Curtis School of Music, Deep Springs (two-year but highly selective), Drury, Gallaudet, Grove City, Howard, Rice College of the Ozarks, Webb Institute of Naval Architecture.

Public two-year community colleges: See pp. 149–151 for information on these very underrated institutions.

U.S. Service Academies: The U.S. Military Academy (West Point), the Naval Academy, the Air Force Academy, the Coast Guard Academy, and the Merchant Marine Academy. Tuition is free, and after graduation, you're guaranteed a job as a military officer. Indeed, you must serve as an officer for four to five years.

Honors programs at an in-state public college: Some top honors programs are listed on pp. 155–156.

Canadian colleges: Heavily subsidized by the government, Canadian colleges are an outstanding value even for non-Canadians, offering high quality and low crime at relatively low cost. Although Americans don't qualify for need-based federal aid at Canadian colleges, they can still take tuition tax credits and U.S. government–subsidized student loans. Some hidden Canadian treasures: Mount Allison, Trent, Acadia, and St. Xavier are top small colleges. Guelph, Waterloo, and Simon Fraser are highly ranked midsized schools, and Queens, McGill, University of Toronto, and University of British Columbia are top universities. Applications for most Canadian colleges are not due until the end of the senior year.

College-within-a-college programs at public colleges: Some are listed on p. 161.

Small public colleges: My favorites include Mary Washington (VA); St. Mary's (MD); New College (FL); California Maritime Academy (CA); Evergreen (WA); College of New Jersey; University of North Carolina, Asheville (NC); and Appalachian State (NC).

Prestigious public colleges: William and Mary; University of Virginia; University of North Carolina, Chapel Hill; University of Michigan; University of California, Los Angeles; University of California, Berkeley; Miami University (OH); University of Texas, Austin.

Prestigious public colleges are among the *worst* values if you have to pay their usually exorbitant out-of-state tuition. To boot, out-of-staters usually get a bad deal on financial aid. (The University of North Carolina, Chapel Hill and the University of Virginia are exceptions according to Kalman Chany, author of *Paying for College Without Going Broke.*)

Colleges offering a three-year bachelor's degree: Finish in three years and you not only save a year's college costs but are in the job market a year earlier, which if you land a job will mean tens of thousands of extra dollars in your pocket. But you have to be a pretty motivated student to do it. Your social and extracurricular life may suffer as well. And you'll probably be taking courses during the summer. Institutions offering three-year bachelor's degrees include Middlebury, Catholic University, Northern Arizona, Southern New Hampshire University (business degree only), Waldorf, and many Canadian colleges.

Private colleges—IF you're likely to get a lot of financial aid. And who is?

— A students applying to colleges that enroll mainly B students.

— Star athletes.

— Students from families that earn less than $80,000.

— African Americans, Hispanics (not from Spain), or Native Americans, especially if their high school record is at least average for that college.

— Students going to schools that are well endowed. For the most part, these are the nationally known brand-name colleges.

— Students going to schools with a track record of generosity. You can compare colleges in their generosity (for example, the percentage of students who get 100 percent of their need met), and what percentage of need is met by grant versus loan at *www.collegeboard.com*. Click on "find a college." Then type in the name of the college you're considering. Also check out the best values list at usnews.com. Click on "America's Best Colleges," then click on "best values."

Okay, readers, I gotta be honest with you. Although I tried to make the rest of this chapter as clear as possible, much of it is still complicated. Worse, it's boring. The good news is that these pages contain keys to saving thousands of dollars. So get up and stretch, take a deep breath, and try to stay with me. I'll make it as simple as possible.

Save for Retirement Before Saving for College

There's money out there for college financial aid, but there is no financial aid for retirement. So, before saving for college, your parents should fully fund any tax-advantaged retirement accounts: 401Ks, 403Bs, and IRAs.

Where to Store the Money You're Saving for College

If your parents' income is less than $60,000 a year, they should consider investing in a no-load growth mutual fund. For specific recommendations, see *Consumer Reports*. A year or two before needing the money, most families move it to a more stable but usually less remunerative investment such as a CD or U.S. Savings Bond. Families too nervous about the volatility of a mutual fund may, from Day One, want to put part or even all money for college into a CD or U.S. Savings Bond.

A lower-risk but likely lower-return option is U.S. Savings Bonds (EE Series issued 1990 or later and all Series I bonds). The interest is excluded from taxable income if used for college tuition and fees (not room and board). For single taxpayers, the tax exclusion phases out for single taxpayers between $58,500 modified adjusted gross income and $73,500. For married taxpayers filing jointly, the phase-out runs from $87,750 to $117,750. The owner of the bond must be 24 or older to qualify for the tax exclusion. The student can be named as the beneficiary, however.

IMPORTANT! If you're unlikely to qualify for financial aid, or if a grandparent or other relative will open the account, seriously consider a 529 *Savings* Plan (not a 529 *Prepaid* Plan). Every state has at least one.

Each 529 Savings Plan offers a range of investment choices: from stocks to bonds to money market investments. Many even offer a guaranteed minimum rate of return (typically at least 3 percent). Beyond the benefits of choice, 529 plans offer tax benefits. They allow your parents or other relative to invest up to $11,000 a year or $55,000 in a lump sum at the beginning of a five-year period. (A married couple can, without incurring gift tax, contribute up to $22,000 a year or $110,000 in the lump sum.) When the money is withdrawn to pay for tuition, room and board or books, all earnings are free of federal tax, and in about half the states, free of state tax.

INSIDER'S SECRET If a relative other than your parent or stepparent opens a 529 account, the assets will not be counted against you when the college calculates how much financial aid you need.

Most people will want to use their own state's 529 plan because it may offer advantages for in-state residents only. If, however, your state's plan doesn't look so hot (for example, if your state plan doesn't offer advantages to in-state residents, or it charges a sales fee or annual expenses over 0.75 percent per year), consider enrolling in an out-of-state plan. Check out *www.savingforcollege.com* for authoritative recommendations.

Apply to a Financial Safety College

Apply to a *financial safety college*, one that one that is very likely to admit you, whose full published price your parents can comfortably afford for at least four years, and that you'd feel okay about attending. For middle incomers, two-year public colleges and four-year in-state public colleges are often smart financial safety colleges.

Apply for Financial Aid—Even If Your Family Has Plenty of Bucks

Many colleges require you to apply for financial aid even if you're just interested in a merit-based (how brilliant or talented you are) scholarship or loan. Besides, the methods for determining financial aid are complex, so you just might get need-based aid even if your family is far from poor. And you'll certainly get a submarket-rate loan. The only time you should **not** apply for financial aid is if **all** of the following are true:

1. You're dying to go to this college AND

2. You doubt you'll be admitted AND

3. Your family can handle the college's published price for at least four years without jeopardizing your family's financial security.

To apply for financial aid, each college will ask your parents to complete one or more forms. (See each college's materials for the specifics.) Just by filling out those only moderately excruciating forms, your family will have applied for more than 95 percent of the available financial aid dollars. Most public colleges ask you just to complete the FAFSA (Free Application for Federal Student Aid), which you can complete and file at *www.fafsa.ed.gov.* A paper version is available at your school in the fall, but the online version is more foolproof. Many private colleges require the FAFSA plus the more in-depth *Profile,* which you can complete and file at *www.profileonline.collegeboard.com.*

If You're Hoping to Get
Need-based Financial Aid

1. **Study hard.** The better your grades and SAT or ACT scores, the more financial aid you're likely to get. This gives a whole new meaning to the advice "Studying pays."

2. **Apply to at least four colleges**, especially if some of them have high sticker prices. (See pp. 20–21 to figure out how many you should apply to.) Financial aid awards can vary wildly from college to college, and if your nth-choice college offers you a wonderful financial aid package, you can use that as ammunition for negotiating a better deal from your first-choice college. Or you and your parents may decide that your nth-choice college is offering too

> **Don't forget to sign the forms. More forms are returned to sender for signature than for any other reason.**

good a deal to pass up. Do not apply to more than ten colleges. It's work for little likely gain, you're likely to do a poorer job on your applications, and come spring, you'll have been admitted to so many colleges, you'll have a hard time making a wise choice.

3. **Try for athletic student aid.** Anna Leider, in *Don't Miss Out*, reports, "You needn't be a star. Just be better than average in a sport, from lacrosse to wrestling. Many colleges seek people who can be developed into varsity material. You may not receive an athletic scholarship, but could get an improved financial aid package."

4. **Meet each college's financial aid application deadlines** because the demand for aid exceeds the supply. For Early Decision and Early Action candidates, the deadline is usually in October or November. For regular applicants, many deadlines are in mid-January to mid-February. Check with each college.

IMPORTANT! Don't wait to file financial aid forms until your parents file their income tax return. Instead, use estimated numbers. If the estimates turn out to be way off, your parent just reports the changes on the Student Aid Report that everyone automatically receives in the spring. Meanwhile, you will have filed the financial aid form(s) by the deadline, and that's what counts.

5. **Don't sound too anxious.** Don't tell the college you're dying to attend it, and think three times before applying Early Decision, which locks you into attending that college. In either case, chances are, you'll get less financial aid. Colleges tend to save their financial aid dollars for students they need to entice. A way to show interest without desperation is to let them know on your application that the college is "among my top choices."

6. **If your brother or sister has thought about going back to college or grad school, a great time to do it is while you're in college.** If your sibling or step-sibling whom your parents deduct on their income tax takes at least six units (usually that's two courses) per term, many colleges will slash your family's expected contribution to college costs in half. This is often true even if the second college student is attending a low-cost community college. Many private colleges are less generous about this. Some colleges will also increase aid if your parent is attending college.

7. **Consider giving a cash gift to your grandparents**. Your financial aid is reduced by 5.6 percent of your parents' assets, 35 percent of your assets, and 0 percent of your grandparents' assets. Without incurring gift tax, a person can give another person up to $11,000 a year. So if two parents give your four grandparents the maximum for just one year, that's $88,000 that won't count against you when the colleges calculate your need for financial aid.

8. **Money should be saved in your parent's name, not yours.** For some reason, colleges give you much less financial aid if savings are in the student's name. If money is already saved in your name,

your family should use that money to pay for your expenses: the orthodontist, a car, or summer camp, for example. You'd think that colleges would encourage students to save money for college. No!

Starting in January of your junior year of high school, don't earn more than $2,490 in one calendar year, including interest or dividends. This is a good time to do the volunteer work or unpaid internship you were considering. Of course, do all the paid work you want if your parents are clearly low-income or make too much to qualify

After the first $2,490 in earnings (including interest and dividends), colleges subtract as much as 85 cents in financial aid from every $1 the student earns and saves!

for financial aid. How do you know? This chart estimates the cash your family will be expected to contribute *each year* to college costs. The estimates are based on a parent age 45, with two kids, one in college. Older parents are expected to pay slightly less. It assumes standard deductions.

9. **Just before the filing date, your parents should prepay taxes, bills, vacations, and so on.** The reason: The forms ask for your family's savings as of the day you file the form.

HOW MUCH WILL COLLEGES EXPECT YOUR FAMILY TO CONTRIBUTE TO COLLEGE COSTS EACH YEAR?

(an estimate for a family of four)[1]

FAMILY ASSETS[2]	FAMILY'S ADJUSTED GROSS INCOME[3]			
	$35,000	$70,000	$105,000	$140,000
$50,000	$2,500	$10,000	$20,000	$31,000
$100,000	$5,000	$13,500	$23,000	$35,000
$150,000	$7,500	$17,000	$26,000	$39,000

[1] If there are three people in your family, add $1,200. If there are five in your family, subtract $1,200, and for each additional person in your family subtract another $1,200.
[2] Not counting your home equity or savings in a retirement account such as an IRA or 401k
[3] Plus any untaxed income

The web site *www.princetonreview.com/college/finance/EFC/* enables you to get a more accurate estimate of how much your family will be expected to contribute to college costs each year. It will generate two estimates: One uses the Federal Methodology. Most public colleges use that number. The other number is based on the Institutional Methodology. That's what most private colleges use.

10. **See if your parents can file a short-form federal tax return.** If your parents have an annual adjusted gross income of less than $50,000 and everyone in your family was eligible to file an IRS Form 1040A or 1040EZ (or wasn't required to file a federal income tax return), your family's assets, no matter how large, won't be counted against you. That could make you eligible for more of the college's grant money, a federal Pell Grant ($4,000 a year) plus a subsidized Stafford Loan (no interest until nine months after you graduate and then low interest, currently about 3 percent).

11. **Your parents should try to maximize their contributions to their retirement plans before January 1 of your junior year.**

12. Your parents should consider **taking capital losses and avoiding capital gains starting January 1 of your junior year in high school through December 31 of your junior year of college.** Capital gains are penalized heavily in the financial aid formula.

13. **Should your divorced parent defer remarrying?** If your divorced parent with whom you live is thinking of remarrying, it may hurt your financial aid. Most colleges consider the income and assets of stepparents-in-residence in assessing how much your family can afford to contribute to college costs. So, many people defer getting married until after their little scholar has graduated from college.

14. **Your generous uncle should not write a check out to you or to the college to help pay for college costs.** To avoid his generosity being penalized by the financial aid formula, he should, **after you graduate college, pay off your student loan.** Or try to convince him that the best way to support your college education is to pay for your spring break in Florida.

15. **Don't overvalue the family business.** If you or your parents own a business, the form will ask for its net worth. Net worth consists only of cash on hand, receivables, furniture, property, and inventory minus accounts payable, debts, and mortgages. It is not the value of the business if you or your parent were to sell it. If your parents have assets that could be used for the business, they're penalized less heavily in the financial aid formula if they're listed as business assets rather than personal assets.

16. **Write a letter to each college's financial aid officer explaining any special circumstances,** for example, your father has lost his job, your parents are divorcing, your parent is planning to retire soon, your family has unusually high housing, medical, or other costs not specified on the forms, or your family income is unusually high this year.

For fuller explanations of these and other financial aid strategies, see the definitive *Paying for College Without Going Broke* or the briefer but also excellent *Don't Miss Out.*

Consider Applying for the Other 5 Percent of Aid

Earlier in this chapter, I said that you apply for at least 95 percent of the financial aid dollars by completing just one or two forms. That 95-plus percent comes from the government and the colleges. The other 5 percent comes from other private sources, such as Mrs. McGillicuddy or the American Golf Caddies Association. Getting a piece of that 5 percent is likely to depend more on your merit than on your neediness.

IMPORTANT! Before fantasizing about your private scholarship, listen to this. If you win one of these scholarships, most colleges will reduce your grant financial aid. These colleges figure, "Great! This kid got $5,000 from someone else. Now she doesn't need our $5,000."

So, if you're applying for financial aid, it's rarely worth all the time and effort to apply for these private scholarships (many have long applications and require an essay and perhaps an out-of-town interview) unless you are confident you'll win big bucks. You may have reason to be confident if you're an academic or extracurricular star plus one of the following: disabled, an "underrepresented" minority, or applying for a scholarship offered by your parent's employer.

If you're still interested in private scholarships, know that their deadlines tend to be in the fall, so if you want freshman money, start looking in spring of your junior year of high school. For local scholarships, check at your high school's college counseling office, local fraternal organizations such as Kiwanis or Rotary, religious institutions, and especially your parent's employer if it's a large organization. For national scholarships, use a no-cost computerized search program such as the one at *www.wiredscholar.com.* Never pay for a scholarship search.

Most students' efforts to land private scholarships yield fewer dollars per hour than they could have earned flipping burgers. So, if you are going to try for private scholarships, apply only for the handful that seem like your best shots. If, however, you're one of your school's stars or are Black, Hispanic, or Native American, and/or are disabled, it's worth applying to ten or 20.

If you win one of these private scholarships, phone your top-choice colleges: "I've received $X,000 from the Kindness Foundation and I'm checking with each college that admitted me to find out whether that will affect my financial aid." That may encourage the colleges to let you keep more of your grant aid. For more on negotiating financial aid, see pp. 91–92.

If Your Family Needs More Money

✓ Take an *unsubsidized* **Stafford Loan, and if necessary, a Plus Loan.** These loans are available to everyone who has applied for financial aid and are ideal for families that don't own a home or don't want to add to their home mortgage. They are unsecured loans, and there's no credit check, so if you can't pay, you won't lose your home.

Subsidized Stafford loans are different only in that your loan doesn't start accruing interest until nine months after you finish your college and graduate school education. Unfortunately, you can get a subsidized Stafford loan only if you qualify for financial aid. Also, your family must pass a credit check.

If the college you attend is a *Direct Lender,* you must obtain your Stafford Loan through the college. If not, shop around. Lenders offer varying discounts. A college's "preferred" lender may not offer you the best deal.

✓ **Consider a home equity line of credit.** The interest is deductible, and it's convenient and economical. Each term, your parent draws out only the amount of money needed to pay your college bills. So, if after your grants, loans, and personal savings, you need only $500 to cover that term's college bill, they just write a check on that line of credit for $500. And because the loan is secured by your home, the interest rate is low. Of course, your parents shouldn't take on too much loan or they could be homeless. Then where would you go to do your laundry?

Other Ways to Cut College Costs

Get college credit without paying tuition

You can earn as much as a year of college credit, thereby saving a year of tuition and room and board, and get your degree a year faster. How? By taking dual-enrollment (college courses for which you get both high school and college credit, available in 20 states), Advanced Placement, or International Baccalaureate courses in high school, and CLEP or PEP exams. (See p. 132 for more information.) Be sure your college awards full credit for these toward the college degree. If your school doesn't offer Advanced Placement courses, you can take them online at *www.apexlearning.com.*

AmeriCorps

Ready for a break between high school and college? Try AmeriCorps, the National Service Program. Volunteer for a year on such projects as housing renovation, child immunization, or neighborhood policing, and you'll not only recharge your batteries and do good, but earn $4,725 toward education costs, $2,362.50 if you do it part time. For more information: *www.americorps.org* or (800) 942-2677.

The Military

The U.S. military academies (army, naval, air force, and don't forget the Coast Guard and Merchant Marines) offer a quality education, an out-of-classroom experience that some many students find extremely rewarding, and a ready-made professional career as a graduation present. And the four-year cost? $0. The hitch? A few-year hitch as a military officer after you graduate college. Phone numbers and web sites are listed on p. 185.

ROTC. A– grades, 1200 on old SAT, a varsity letter, and willingness to consider a military career can land you a scholarship that pays part or all tuition and books at many colleges, possibly for four years. You'll spend five to 15 hours a week on military coursework and intense physical and leadership training, including marching on campus, perhaps to the jeers of campus radicals. You'll also commit to a few years in the active or reserve military after college. If you're male, you'll be required to get a haircut you'll never forget. For information go to *www.armyrotc.com* (army) *www.nrotc.navy.mil* (navy and marines), or *www.afrotc.com* (air force). Or call (800) USA ROTC (army), (800) NAV-ROTC (navy or marines), (800) 423-USAF (air force.)

Have your parents buy a house or condo near the college.

You live there and rent it to other students. Because all expenses are tax deductible and because good real estate in college towns tends to appreciate, your housing costs could be much less than if you lived in the dorm. You might even make a profit.

After You've Heard from the Colleges

Compare financial aid awards from each college:

✓ How much cash will your family have to come up with? Don't forget about the costs of travel to and from school plus, the $5,000–$8,000 a year in living expenses most students incur, for dates, road trips with friends, clothes, trips back home, and so on. CAUTION: Be sure your family will be able to afford to make the payments for at least four years. (Many students take five or six.) You'd feel terrible if somewhere along the line, your family said, "We're out of money. You have to drop out."

✓ Even if your family does its part, will the college? As long as your family's income stays the same, will your cash award be renewed each year, or once they gotcha, will they pull the plug?

For example, *US News and World Report* reported the case of Laura Ng, who chose to enroll at the University of Maine, Orono, because it offered her a full scholarship. After the first year, she was informed she would be required to take on an $8,000 loan just to pay for her sophomore year at this state university. Peggy Crawford, the university's financial aid director, lamely explained, "Our goal is for students to receive the same dollars but we can't guarantee the same package."

A college is especially likely to turn off its financial aid spigot if you take more than four years to graduate. Imagine that in year five or six, after all that effort, you couldn't graduate because the college stopped your financial aid. Find out which colleges won't abandon you.

Often your financial aid award letter will not provide such information. Call to find out and get the answer in writing.

✓ How big a loan will you have to pay back? Beware: Some colleges include **un**subsidized Stafford and Plus loans in the "financial aid" package. This is misleading. Those loans are not financial aid; they are available to everyone, even zillionaires.

✓ If you applied Early Decision or Early Action, will your award be increased to cover the next year's tuition increase?

IMPORTANT! If your award from your top-choice college seems too low, or you've gotten a better deal from another college, **negotiate (or better, or have your parent negotiate) a better deal with the financial aid office. The key is to provide new information that can justify a new decision**.

You might explain that other colleges have offered you a better deal. (Now you see why I want you to apply to at least four colleges, especially colleges that compete with each other for students?) A tactful approach: "I'd like to attend your college but I just can't justify spending $3,000 more *each year* than it would cost to attend College B." Or ask, "Could you *reevaluate* my package?" Don't use the word "negotiate." Colleges don't like the implication that their price is fluid. If true, explain that your family's financial picture isn't as rosy as the financial aid form made it appear. Perhaps your parent's salary or bonus has been cut, your aging grandparent will require money, your brother will soon be headed for college, your sister was suffering in the too-gritty public school and so must attend private high school, or your home badly needs major repairs. Sometimes, sending an itemized budget to the financial aid officer can make your family's situation clearer. Finally, send copies of letters of recommendation from teachers, counselors, coaches, or your boss, explaining what a deserving soul you are.

In College

At college, you can do a lot to ease your financial stress.

Land your work-study job early

If your financial aid package includes a work-study job, your first stop on campus should be to the student employment office. The good jobs go fast. Procrastinate and you may find yourself mopping floors. Some of the most rewarding and scarce jobs are assisting a professor in your prospective major. Ask the department secretary for leads.

IMPORTANT! Income from work-study jobs, which are awarded as part of your financial aid package, do not count against you when the college computes your financial aid for the next year.

Other part-time jobs

Some of the more rewarding options include tutoring (get clients by placing signs on campus bulletin boards), coaching students to use computers more effectively, and owning a cart that sells espresso, sandwiches, and/or desserts next to campus. You might even offer financial aid counseling. If you really understand everything in this chapter plus that in *Don't Miss Out* or *Paying for College Without Going Broke*, you're ahead of many financial aid advisors who hang out a shingle.

IMPORTANT! If you're getting financial aid, keep your earnings (not counting any work-study job) under $2,490 a year because the college will likely reduce your next year's financial aid by 50 to 85 percent of what you earned and saved above $2,490.

Check your first college invoice

Be sure your first bill includes all the financial aid the college promised you. If if doesn't, contact the billing office.

Open a checking account

Choose a bank with a branch within walking distance of your dorm room. It should also be convenient to your parents' bank or at least on the same ATM system (Star, Honor, Cirrus, Plus) so it's easy for them to fatten your account. Keep enough money in your account to cover all the checks you write for books, tuition, utilities, and midnight pizza.

As soon as you write a check or make a deposit or withdrawal, write it in the check register that comes with your checkbook. You will, however, at some point, make the classic college student financial move: write a check for 34 cents. And bounce it.

The Secret to Being a Happy Credit Card User

The interest rate on credit cards, especially those offered to young adults, can approach Vito the Shark's. Charge only as much as you can afford to pay each month. Paying interest gives you no pleasure at all and costs you plenty. And don't be like the 20 percent of college students who carry four or more credit cards.

Some credit cards offer a good deal for college students or for the college-bound. A major bank's card will put at least 1% of your purchases into an account, which you may transfer into a 529 account. A leading mutual fund's credit card credits 2% of all purchases into a special account. Both credit cards have income requirements, so in most cases, your parents will need to apply for the card. Deals change so it's best to check into the various cards currently available.

Other money savers

✓ If attending an out-of-state public college, you may be wondering if you can qualify for in-state tuition. Probably not. In many states, it used to be easy. In Oklahoma, you'd walk into the financial aid office on the first day of school and say, "Hi, I'm a Sooner," and you'd be declared an Oklahoma resident for tuition purposes. Now, most states have clamped down. Nevertheless, it's worth asking the financial aid office how students can qualify for the in-state tuition rate. In a few states, all you may have to do is register your car, vote in that state, and indicate, if it's true, that you plan to live in the state after you graduate.

✓ **Take advantage of the government's Hope Scholarship.** Your family can get a tax credit of $1,500 for tuition paid during each of your first two years of college. (This phases out for couples with $83,000–$103,000 in adjusted gross income and for single parents earning $41,000–$51,000.)

✓ For the third, fourth, and fifth years of college, families can **claim a Lifetime Learning Tax Credit** of 20 percent of the first $10,000 of tuition and fees, up to $2,000 per family.

✓ If your family makes too much money to qualify for the Hope or Lifetime credits, they can deduct up to $4,000 in tuition expenses if your family's adjusted gross income is below $130,000 ($65,000 for single filers). They can deduct up to $2,000 if your family income is between $130,000 and $160,000, or if single with income between $65,000 and $80,000.

✓ Your parents can also deduct up to $2,500 in college loan interest. This deduction phases out for joint filers with incomes between $100,000 and $130,000, single filers with incomes between $50,000 and $65,000.

✓ If midyear your family's finances change, contact the financial aid office. Funds are available for such situations.

✓ Most students do their scholarship searching before getting into college but there's money for nonfreshmen that may be worth going for. See the financial aid office and the chair of your major department, and do a free scholarship search on *www.wiredscholar.com.*

Why Is College So Darned Expensive?

Colleges keep raising tuition. According to the College Board, average family income has increased only 10 percent in the past decade, but the average college tuition has increased 43 percent. The published price (plus a fair estimate of living expenses) for four years at a brand-name private college now averages $180,000.

For decades, private colleges have been increasing tuition well beyond the inflation rate, but now even brand-name state universities have joined the game. Here were some of the increases for the 2003–04 school year, a year in which the inflation rate was just 2 percent: Ohio State 19 percent; University of Iowa 19 percent; University of Virginia 20 percent; University of North Carolina, Chapel Hill 21 percent; State University of New York 28 percent; University of California 30 percent; Arizona State 40 percent.

Why the skyrocketing costs? State budgets are strapped and must hit the students. Also, colleges increasingly want to play Robin Hood: forcing students and families to pay an inflated tuition rate to subsidize low-income students—forced charity.

How can colleges get away with charging what would seem to be an unaffordable amount? Because the government is using taxpayer money to vastly increase financial aid through Hope Scholarships, Lifetime Learning Credits, subsidized Stafford Loans, increased Pell Grants, and so on. That makes college more affordable for students, so colleges can afford to raise tuition. So, ironically, when the government provides more financial aid, the beneficiary is not the student, it's the colleges—they can and do raise tuition!

Why is no one asking colleges to be more efficient? For example, should professors really be earning a full-time salary for teaching just two or three classes per semester? (Three classes per **year** at my alma mater, U.C. Berkeley!) Why aren't interactive-video-based, simulation-based courses taught by the nation's best professors being used instead of large lecture classes? That would raise quality while lowering cost.

When your electric company wants to raise the price of a kilowatt a dime, a government oversight body holds endless hearings. It's on the front page of the newspaper. Yet colleges, year after year, raise prices beyond the rate of inflation, and we don't blink.

Even entities that don't get our tax dollars get more scrutiny than colleges do. When a number of accidents occurred that appeared to be the result of defective tires, the media was relentless in attacking the tire manufacturer, so much so that many observers doubt it can stay in business. Colleges charge enormous sums of money to produce, day in and day out, huge quantities of defective products—students who either don't graduate or if they do, have shockingly poor reading, writing, and thinking skills. Yet we continue to accept that and give them—public and private colleges—ever more of our tax dollars.

The media and our government must be smarter and start treating colleges as they treat other businesses. Perhaps we should revoke their status as nonprofit organizations. We certainly should demand from colleges the same degree of accountability that we do from tire manufacturers.

Only if we stop viewing academe as an unassailable sacred cow can we even hope that a college education can improve from being one of America's most overpriced products to becoming the national treasure we believe it is.

Remember!

1. Except in some parts of the South and the Midwest, the sticker price of a bachelor's degree obtained in four years (and only 37 percent finish in four years) at a brand-name public college (in state) averages $90,000, at a brand-name private $180,000. And even if you qualify for financial aid, an average of only 39 percent of that is grant. The rest is interest-bearing loan and a low-paying work-study job.

2. The easiest, most powerful way to make college affordable is to choose a college with a low published (sticker) price. Don't worry, research finds that attending a less expensive college does *not* mean a lower-quality education or worse career prospects.

3. Always apply to at least one financial safety college—one whose published price your family can comfortably afford for four years without jeopardizing the family's financial security.

4. For most families with incomes of at least $50,000 a year, consider saving for college in a 529 Savings Plan, especially if a relative other than a parent will open it. First check your state's 529 Plan. If you have to pay a sales fee to buy it or the annual expenses are more than 3/4 of one percent a year, check out other plans.

5. Even if your family is far from poor, apply for financial aid. Many colleges award aid based on your merit, not your financial need, as well as no-need loans, but require you to complete the financial aid forms.

6. You apply for more than 95 percent of all financial aid by filling out just one or two forms: usually the FAFSA for public schools, and in addition, the Profile at private schools. To see which forms you need, visit the web sites of the colleges to which you are applying.

7. If you're applying for financial aid, apply for admission to at least four colleges. Financial aid awards can vary wildly from college to college, and if your nth-choice college offers you a wonderful financial aid package, you can use that as the basis for negotiating a better deal from your first-choice college.

8. If you're likely to be financial aid eligible (check at *www.princeton review.com/college/finance/EFC/*), money to pay for your college education should be saved in your parents' or relative's names, not yours. The financial aid formula heavily penalizes student earnings and savings.

9. Applying for the 5 percent of other college money—private scholar-ships—is generally worth the effort only if you're a true campus star, disabled, or are Black, Latino, or Native American. Otherwise, you probably could make more money per hour working at McDonalds. Never pay for a private scholarship search. Use one of the free ones such as *www.wiredscholar.com.*

10. Carefully compare your financial aid awards from each college. How much cash will you have to come up with that first year? Will they guarantee that, if your family's income remains the same, you'll get the same amount the following years? Even in that fifth year that most students take? Or will the college, after the first year or after the fourth, turn the financial aid spigot down or off so it can use the money to entice more freshmen?

11. If your financial aid award seems too low, ask a college admissions officer to "reevaluate" (not "negotiate") your package based on new information: a better package offered by another college, a change in your family's financial situation, or additional information that makes clearer that it would be difficult for your family to afford that college with so little cash financial aid.

12. Take advantage of the many tax breaks available to soften the blow of college costs: Hope Scholarship, Lifetime Learning Credit, tuition deduction, and college loan interest deduction.

The Keys to a Great College Experience

Sharing a bathroom with 16 strangers, half of them guys?
You gotta be kidding!
—Jennifer, Bishop O'Dowd H.S., Oakland, CA.

Ready for the most important statement in this entire book? Here goes: The key to a great college experience is not where you go, it's what you do there. You can have a miserable experience at Harvard and a wonderful one at No-Name State. The good news is that if you handle the 22 decisions in this chapter well, you're almost guaranteed a great college experience. And you'll probably graduate.

Think graduating is no big deal? Think again. In the freshman year alone, 25 percent of students drop out or transfer. And if you were admitted because you're an athlete, child of an alum, or under an affirmative action program, you're at even greater risk. Don't just read this chapter. Study it as if it were the textbook for the most important test you've ever taken. It is.

If you like, don't read about all 22 decisions now. Just flip through the headings and pick one or two that intrigue you. Then keep this book on your bookshelf at college to be called on as needed.

I'm Leaving for College Soon. Help!

CRITICAL DECISION #1:
WHERE SHOULD I LIVE?

Top Eight Characteristics of On-campus Housing

1. You get to live with lots of other freshmen. It's fun to live with people in the same boat as you are.

2. You live in a cinder-block room so small that it would be illegal to house a welfare recipient there. And you have to share it with another student. Maybe two. And then there's the bathroom you have to share with 16 other freshmen with questionable sanitary habits.

3. Dorm[1] life is a crash course in how to get along with anyone, from cretins to goddesses.

4. It's easier to get involved in campus activities when they're just steps away.

5. It's a good way to make close friends. Often dorm friends move to an off-campus apartment, and have been known, 40 years later, to call each other and reminisce about the good ol' days.

6. There's always something going on in the dorm—a bull session, party, study group—whether you want it or not.

7. Classroom buildings are usually within walking distance. If your college is frozen from December through March, this *will* matter to you.

8. Eating is easy: all-you-can-eat buffets three times a day, and you don't have to lift a finger other than the one holding your fork. Of course, three buffets every day can easily cause the Freshman 10, the typical weight gain. To avoid it, you'll probably need to make friends with salads, fruits and veggies, and nonfat frozen yogurt. Don't worry—an occasional hot fudge topping won't turn you into a blimp.

---

[1] The more accurate, if awkward, term is "residence hall."

A dorm is not a dorm is not a dorm. A regular dorm, especially one with lots of freshmen, often isn't the "living-learning environment" described in college propaganda. It can be pretty rowdy, and you may find it's hard to study or sleep there. But there are ways to cope with the situation, and you can always move.

You may roll your eyes, but please consider a dorm that attracts non-maniacs: the quiet, academic, foreign language, honors dorms, and especially living-learning programs (see pp. 160–161). Many students avoid these dorms, envisioning nerd-filled rooms in a monastery-like environment. The truth is that students in these dorms usually have balanced lives: weeknights are generally quiet and weekends are generally social. If you want to find fun, it's usually just steps away, but it's nice to be able to count on times when you can study or sleep in your room. Combine the balanced atmosphere with the better students these residence halls attract plus their special extracurricular programming, and it's easy to see how these dorms can be key to a good college experience.

INSIDER'S SECRET Another key to avoiding unwanted noise is to request a dorm room away from the hall telephone, bathroom, entrance/exit door, or parking lot.

WARNING! Your student housing contract isn't exactly ironclad. More than a few universities have had problems fulfilling room-and-board promises. Mark Robillard, director of housing at pricey Boston University says, "We don't want to turn people away, but you just can't create beds."[2] Inquiring minds want to know why the heck do colleges admit more students than they can house?

The university sob story doesn't make displaced students feel any better. "We came home and found a guy living in our room's lounge. He was there for two weeks without any notice," says Hofstra freshman Scott Span. Many colleges have turned to hotels and the local YMCA to ease overcrowding.[3]

---

[2] *U Magazine,* Sept. 1997
[3] Ibid.

Top Four Characteristics of Apartment Life

1. No random roommates. You live with whom you want.

2. You have more space for your junk.

3. Costs are higher. Don't forget hidden costs like heating in winter, transportation to campus, and parking, which Worthington and Farrar[4] describe as "the nightmare that never ends."

4. If you live off-campus, it's easy to miss out on the full college experience. You'll have to make extra efforts to get involved in campus activities.

Top Six Characteristics of Living at Home

1. Your family saves a few thousand bucks each year.

2. You miss out on the intermediate step between the protection of home and the responsibility of living on your own.

3. You may have more spacious surroundings: like your own room plus a living room.

4. You may be able to get home-cooked meals, custom-tailored to your taste.

5. It's easier to do laundry, and it may even be done for you.

6. With fewer distractions and a nagging parent, you may be more likely to get your assignments done.

A Good Compromise

Spend a semester or year in the dorm, then move to a near-campus apartment with a friend or two. If money is a problem and home is nearby, move back home. Or take a job as a live-in nanny or elder

---

[4] Janet F. Worthington and Ronald T. Farrar, *The Ultimate College Survival Guide* (Princeton, N.J.: Peterson's, 1998). As you'll see, I frequently cite this guide; it's worth a spot on your bookshelf. And these great sites won't even take up any space on your bookshelf: *www.cybercampus.com* and *www.collegeclub.com*.

companion. Even one term on campus will give you the experience of having gone off to college.

Room with Your Best Friend from High School?

This is usually not a good idea. Of course, you can stay friends, but rooming together too often messes up the friendship or keeps both of you from meeting other people.

CRITICAL DECISION #2: SHOULD I GO TO ORIENTATION?

Don't miss it! It has been said that missing orientation is like not reading the owner's manual. There are activities to help students get to know each other and the campus. For example, a small group of new-comers led by a senior usually explores the campus together and learns how to make the most of the place—everything from how to get football tickets to how to get good profs, from where the jobs are to where the romantic spots are.

CRITICAL DECISION #3: WHEN SHOULD I SHOW UP ON CAMPUS?

First days can be overwhelming so plan to arrive on campus as early as possible. Ask your roommate to do the same. By meeting each other early, on the off chance you hate each other, there's time for a switch before classes start. While you're on the phone with your roommate, agree about who's going to bring what. No need for two popcorn poppers.

Other advantages of arriving early: the best student jobs go early, more time to meet friends, and you get textbooks before the bookstore line gets out of control.

"Buh-bye, Mom and Dad." Now What?

CRITICAL DECISION #4:
AM I GOING TO BE SERIOUS
ABOUT MANAGING MY TIME?

You're going to be free! Your own boss! You'll decide how you'll spend every minute of every day—whether you like it or not.

There are two keys to time management: Having a good system and sticking to it. I'll cover both right now.

Keys to Managing Your Time Well

Follow Ben Franklin. Early morning has the fewest distractions. So you'll be able to fit tons more stuff into a day if you can, by any chance—and few young people can—follow Ben's advice: "Early to bed, early to rise, makes you healthy, wealthy, and wise." Then again, Ben probably never rushed a fraternity.

Use a Week-at-a-Glance pocket calendar. Enter everything: due dates for term papers, the basketball game, appointment for meeting with profs, the TV special, your family members' and Sweetie's birthday. For term papers and projects, mark the date you need to start working on them—a good way to prevent No-Doz all-nighters.

> Time is your most valuable commodity. So, just for the first few weeks at college until you get into the habit, please learn how to make the most of your time. You'll be halfway home to a great college experience.

Most important, keep a daily to-do list in your pocket calendar, and check it first thing each morning. Make it a habit. Keep it with you all day. As something gets done, cross it off. It will feel good. As you think of something you need to do, do it right then or write it down.

Beware of the tube. Martin Spethman, in *How to Get Into and Graduate from College in Four Years*, only half-joking says, "If you never pick up a remote control during college, your chances of graduating in four years double."

Use dead time. There are many bits of dead time during each day—when you're in line, in between classes, on the bus, waiting for a late professor to show up, the ten minutes until your favortie TV show comes on. If you always keep a book or notebook computer with you, you can get hours of work done without giving up a single fun activity.

Take short breaks. Long breaks from studying are big time drains. You can often clear your head quickly with a one-minute break. If that doesn't work, try three minutes. Wanna try a little compulsivity? Set a timer to avoid three minutes turning into 20.

Limit a paying job to 10 to 20 hours a week. Most students can hold a paying job for as many as 10–20 hours a week and still succeed as a full-time student. If you need to work more than 20 hours, see your college's financial aid officer. You may be able to wring a few extra bucks from the college coffers.

These final two suggestions will help you develop a personalized time management system. Each requires a one-time effort, but it will probably be worth it, especially if you have a history of not getting stuff done.

Discover how you really spend your time. For one week, everywhere you go, carry a memo pad and a watch or timer that you can set to go off every 15 minutes. (You can get one for $5 to $10.) Each time it beeps, write what you're doing at that moment. At the end of the week, look over your memo pad. Most students decide to rearrange their priorities.

For example, Mark, a Southwest Missouri State freshman, found that every day he took a ten-minute walk down to the gym to play basketball for a couple of hours. That's 17 hours a week, 17 percent of his waking hours—not counting the shower. He decided that was too much. So, now, most of the time, he rides an exercise bike in his dorm (just a one-minute walk from his room) while reading a textbook 30 minutes five days a week, the amount that's supposed to give you maximum benefit for minimal effort. That one change saved Mark 14 hours a week! Plus, he gets some of his studying done.

Take control of your life. Make copies of the scheduling chart on the next page. Fill in your schedule for the coming week. Then *follow it.* Some people think that following a schedule will restrict your freedom, but it's the opposite. By confining your coursework to your favorite work times, you'll have more time for fun, and those hours won't be spoiled by the guilt of knowing you should be studying.

- ✓ First, block in your classes (and ideally a few minutes before and after class for reviewing your notes)

- ✓ Next, insert recreation times you know you don't want to give up

- ✓ Fill in your prime times for studying (15 to 25 hours a week if you're a typical full-time student). Prime times are the hours that you're fresh enough to concentrate and least likely to be distracted. These prime times are critical. Nothing should pull you away from your desk during prime times—except maybe that great party you're dying to go to.

My Schedule

	Mon.	Tues.	Wed.	Thurs.	Fri.	Sat.	Sun.
7 A.M.							
8							
9							
10							
11							
12							
1 P.M.							
2							
3							
4							
5							
6							
7							
8							
9							
10							

Now that you have a time-management system, don't let procrastination keep you from using it. Here's how. Actually, let's postpone this part for later. Just kidding.

Cures for the Average Procrastinator

Remind yourself of the benefits of getting the task done. They include higher grades; not feeling guilty that you didn't get it done, better writing, reading, and math skills that will help you all your life.

Think back to times you didn't procrastinate. What were the outcomes? Positive, I'll bet.

Just do it. Do it now, even if you don't feel like it. If you only study when you feel like it, you won't feel like it often enough. Fight the discomfort, and just do it. If you're really brave, start with your most difficult assignment first.

Getting started is sometimes the hardest part. So think how great it will feel to have put in a good half-hour. Then literally force yourself to sit down, and ask yourself, **"What is the first tiny thing I have to do?"** For example, "I have to open my assignment book to see what pages I have to read." That can get you rolling.

TRUTH: The more you accomplish, the more you want to accomplish. The less you accomplish, the less you want to accomplish. And it only continues as you get older. You will not wake up when you're 40 and suddenly decide you're willing to work hard.

Be aware of the moment of truth. When you get to that first hard part, I know it's tempting to sharpen your pencil, grab a Coke or, call your girlfriend. That's the moment you have to force yourself to stay with the task. **Give yourself a one-second task.** One second is a totally unintimidating amount of time. Often, that one-second task will get you rolling again.

Don't think about how much work you have ahead of you. That can overwhelm you into procrastination. Instead, think like a mountain climber. Just put one foot in front of the other, and when you get to the top and look down, you'll be amazed at how far you've gone.

Only struggle for a minute. After that, get help, decide you can skip it, or come back to it later. Struggling with something for more than a minute usually results in frustration and you end up getting much less done.

Create an artificial deadline. Do you wait until the last minute because you need time pressure to motivate you? Create an artificial deadline. For example, hand your roommate $20. If you don't finish the task by the agreed-on time, she keeps your 20 bucks.

For the Professional Procrastinator

Serious procrastinators feel like a car trying to move with the emergency brake on. Here are some ways to start zooming again.

Hedonism. Some people procrastinate to avoid the pain of work. They forget that procrastination causes much more pain—the ongoing guilt about not having started and the pain that comes from the lower grades procrastination causes. Someone once said that procrastination is like a credit card—fun to use, painful when the bill comes in. The truly hedonistic approach is to get the work done as quickly as reasonably possible, so maximum time is left for pleasure, without any guilt or negative consequences to spoil the fun.

Fear of failure. Many serious procrastinators fear failure. Subconsciously they think, "If I don't try, I can't fail." The procrastinator convinces herself, "I could have done it, but I just decided not to try."

> **Not trying is the one thing that guarantees failure, the one thing that ensures you'll be perceived as a loser.**

The cure is to recognize that not trying ensures far greater failure. The fact is, most successful people fail a lot. The difference between winners and losers is how they react to failing. Winners don't waste time on self-pity. They simply learn from their failure so they're more likely to succeed the next time. Even Hall of Fame baseball players have slumps, but they don't sulk. They figure out what bad habit they've gotten into and keep trying to fix it until they're hitting home runs again.

Fear of success. Serious procrastination can also come from the opposite—fear of success: "If I do well here, I'll be expected to do even more in the future."

The cure for this is to remember that you can set limits. For example, many successful executives have decided that the stressful 70-hour weeks aren't worth it no matter how high the salary, and quit and do something low-key such as teaching in college.

Resenting authority. Serious procrastination can come from resenting authority (the professor): "You're not going to make me do that." You're right. No one can make you do anything. But if you make the choice not to do coursework, it's you, not the authority, who will suffer. Ask yourself this: Why am I paying thousands of dollars to do nothing?

PARENTAL NOTE If your child is an inveterate procrastinator, ask if he thinks it would be helpful to phone you every day to give a progress report. Regular check-in is a key to the success of Weight Watchers and 12-step programs.

CRITICAL DECISION #5: AM I GOING TO GET ALONG WITH MY ROOMMATE?

You may never again have to spend so much time with someone with so few feet of space between you. If they put a welfare recipient in a college dorm, the ACLU would probably sue, claiming it's inhumane to make two or three people live in such cramped quarters.

Yet the most helpful advice can be summarized in two words: *be nice.* You're probably nice much of the time naturally. With a roommate you just have to be nice more often. But nice doesn't mean doormat. You and your roommates might want to complete the following document.

ROOMMATE BILL OF RIGHTS

All roommates have the right to

✓ a room that is clean enough. We will define "clean enough" as:

✓ a part of the room that is each person's own. We will separate our room in this way:

✓ expect that roommates will respect personal belongings. Our rule about borrowing will be:

✓ host guests at agreed-on times, with guests respecting the rights of the host, roommates, and other hall residents. The following times are appropriate to host guests:

✓ study free from noise. The following times will be reserved for quiet study:

✓ sleep without noise. Quiet will prevail after the following times:

✓ expect fairness regarding the telephone. Our rule about use of the phone and paying the bill is:

✓ expect that all disagreements will be discussed openly and with respect and that it is acceptable, when any roommate feels it is necessary, to involve a residence hall staff member in the discussion.

We, the undersigned, agree to all of the above. Additionally, we agree that this agreement may be changed by mutual agreement of all roommates.

Signatures:

Date:

If there's a problem, don't stew; talk to your roommate about it. It's amazing how many conflicts you'll avoid just by saying, "Could you please stop sneaking your dirty clothes into my laundry hamper?" You'll have a better chance of getting your roommate's attention if you preface your request with, "There's something important I want to talk with you about. Is this a good time?"

Start with a diplomatic opening line such as, "I hope this isn't a stupid question," "Please forgive me for asking," or "I need a big favor."

> **Remember, though, what Tolstoy said, "Everyone thinks of changing humanity. No one thinks of changing themselves."**

Everyone messes up occasionally, but what if despite repeated tactful reminders and compromising, your roommate and you can't work things out? Remember, you're paying good money to attend this college, and that entitles you to a reasonable roommate. Speak with your resident assistant, the older student who is paid to live in your dorm to handle problems like this. If that doesn't fix the problem, insist on a new roommate, or move.

You can increase your odds of being happy with your roommate by being really honest when completing the roommate-matching questionnaire that you'll receive when first admitted to college. If you are an incorrigible partier, don't say you're quiet just because it sounds better.

What Am I Going to Do for Fun?

CRITICAL DECISION #6:
WILL I MAKE FRIENDS?

It can be scary. Away from home for four whole years! What if you don't make friends? What if you're so lonely that you call home twice a day? What if you end up spending every spare moment watching stupid TV shows because there's no one to do anything with?

Not to worry. You'll be around thousands of other students eager to meet new people, and you'll have endless opportunities to meet them: classes, games, parties, exercising, lines, meals, and so on.

I interviewed dozens of students who made lots of friends to discover the secrets to their success. Laurie's story summarized what I learned:

I know how to make friends because my Army family relocated so often. I was kind of nervous when I arrived at college, but I knew that all the other freshmen probably were too, so I immediately started conversations with just about anyone who looked nice. I met them in all sorts of places—in class (I made a point of showing up a few minutes early), in one of those lines you're always in at college, in the dining hall, at the chemistry majors club, in the orchestra (which I immediately joined—a great place to meet people), at a student mixer in the dorm, in the library (a very cute guy I made sure to sit across from), on the jogging trail, in the student union, during intramural volleyball, in the laundry room. The laundry room is a great place to meet people—you've got nothing to do but talk for a half hour.

You'd be amazed how approachable people are, even the gorgeous ones. Most people are mirrors—if you notice they aren't smiling or being friendly to you, they're probably responding to the way you're acting. Smile!

Don't wait for someone to start talking to you. You can start a conversation by talking about almost anything: "Gee, this is a long line." "That was an interesting class." "You a freshman, too?" "How's the burrito?"

Once the conversation started, I tried to really listen well and then ask a follow-up question or comment that built on what they said. I might ask about their classes, where they're from, what made them choose this college, the dorm, their family, or what activities they do in college. If I wanted to develop a friendship, next I'd say, "Hey maybe we can get together sometime. Can I have your phone number?" Then I'd phone and say something like, "Listen, I gotta do my laundry. Wanna keep me company?" or "I've had enough studying. Wanna go down to the snack bar?" Right before school started, I threw a back-to-the-grind party and invited my entire dorm floor. Pretty soon, I had a nice network of friends.

Of course, making friends is too complicated to be reduced to a formula, but someone who has just arrived at college may not know where to begin. Laurie's way can help ensure you won't spend four years in solitary confinement.

Laurie was pretty assertive. But what if you're shy? Worthington and Farrar offer this advice: Leave your dorm room door open and keep music on. Read the campus newspaper every day and look for interesting upcoming events and meetings. (And go!) If you're feeling left out, drop in on your dorm's resident advisor or make an appointment to see a counselor at the student counseling center. Many college students feel sad at times, and college counselors have lots of experience in helping.

No matter what your approach, start early. Those first few weeks are when everyone is looking to meet people. If you lock yourself up in your room waiting for someone to drop in, you'll blow a great chance at a social life, and your dorm neighbors might think you're stuck up or want to be left alone.[5]

CRITICAL DECISION #7:
WHO WILL BE MY CLOSE FRIENDS?

This is impossible to reduce to a few words, but consider this. Choose friends who help you to be your best self, not those who seem disappointed by your success or try to drag you down with them. If they give you more anxiety than energy, look elsewhere. Of course, you, too, should try to help your friends be their best selves.

CRITICAL DECISION #8
WILL I HAVE A GOOD ROMANTIC LIFE?

"First of all, lighten up. . . Don't look at everyone as a potential girlfriend or boyfriend, and don't think of every person you date as your future mate for life."[6] College really is a good time to make friends with

---

[5] Worthington and Farrar, *Ultimate College Survival Guide.*
[6] Ibid.

and date a number of people. When it's time, the right one will drop out of the sky. Think that, anyway.

And women, do you like a guy? Don't wait helplessly like the passive females of the '50s. Ask him out, if you want.

Avoiding AIDS and Other Nasties

Abstinence ain't bad. Plenty of intimacy and fun is possible without the risk of AIDS, other sexually transmitted diseases, and, of course, pregnancy.

If you do choose to have intercourse, a strict "no glove, no love" policy is the best way to minimize the risks that go along with sex. Condoms pack a one-two punch, preventing both STD's and unwanted pregnancies. You're in college, which presumably means you're smart, so don't make a stupid mistake that could change the rest of your life. Even if you've been with someone for months and have been tested, condoms are still a good idea.

Many guys hate wearing condoms. Under the influence of alcohol or drugs, even many nice guys will downplay the risk to avoid having to wear one. Besides, he may not know that one of his previous partners slept with someone who is HIV positive. You're not just having sex with your partner; you're sleeping with every other person your partner has ever slept with.

Avoiding Date Rape

A word to girls: If you're not sure you can trust your partner, and especially if either of you is under the influence, don't be in a private place. And if you've been dumb enough to ignore that advice, and you mean NO, you must make it plain. That means, when he goes too far, you stand up, and in a strong voice, say, "I said no." (This is tough if you're under the influence.)

A word to guys: Neanderthal days are over. Push

> **Many guys interpret a half-hearted "no" while you're still lying there as "Convince me." If you mean "maybe," don't say no. Your partner is not a mind reader. If you give an unclear message, it's probably unfair of you to yell "date rape" the next morning.**

yourself where you're not wanted, and not only are you being unfair, every woman will soon think of you as "that jerk." Women talk with each other. A lot. If she wants you, she will, at least in nonverbal ways, let you know. Besides, the legal tables have turned. On many college campuses, right or wrong, if a woman charges date rape or sexual harassment, you're often presumed guilty until proven innocent. Unfair but true.

CRITICAL DECISION #9: "HEY, WANNA GET WASTED?"

I can hear you thinking, "Oh no. Not another lecture about drinking and drugs!" Sorry, but I couldn't feel good about writing a college guide without saying something about it.

IMPORTANT! The most depressing thing I've found in my years of working with college and college-bound students is how, even at prestigious colleges, many students waste away their college years and may even mess up their entire lives because of alcohol or drugs. For them, college is the world's most expensive cover charge. Thousands of college students say, "I can handle it," and by the time they realize they can't, it's too late. So, I feel compelled to tell you a little of what I've learned from talking with lots of students.

It's not surprising that students drink or smoke marijuana at college. Alcohol or pot may provide a way to relax, feel cool, and avoid being judged as if you were on your best behavior. And the booze companies spend millions to brainwash you into thinking that alcohol unlocks the door to happiness. But picture a half gallon of beer sloshing around in you. Imagine other students looking at you sitting there stoned and thinking what a loser you are.

These visions appeal to few students, yet some get stoned or drunk every week or even more. Especially if they hang out with other losers, it's easy to drink or smoke away four years of social life without realizing what they've done. If they graduate, they will have made worse friends and missed out on the best parts of college life.

This is not a plea for abstinence. It's a request for conscious choice. I know it's hard to set a limit, but try to—in advance—decide if and approximately how much you want to drink. Unless you have an addictive personality, there may be nothing wrong with a drink or two (if it's legal) to take the edge off or to quell a bit of nervousness at a party. But much more than that can reduce your social life to hovering over a toilet, acting like an ass, or passing out and missing the fun. It can turn you into a permanent loser and maybe even cost you your life in a car accident.

It goes without saying that drinking and driving is beyond stupid, as is riding with someone who has been drinking. Get a cab or remember to assign a designated driver—someone who agrees not to drink for the night *and* sticks to the agreement. Also, many campuses have safe-ride programs.

There's good news. "You may be pleasantly surprised to find out that there is less peer pressure to drink or do drugs in college than there was in high school. If you just tell the truth and say you'd rather have a Coke, it won't matter to most people."[7]

You won't have a problem if you stay away from people who frequently get drunk and from parties where the main objective is to get loaded. Do you really want to be friends with them anyway? At a party, hang out with the unstoned. They may not be as obvious as the big boozers, but most parties have them, and they do have fun. Some camouflage themselves by nursing a beer for an hour or sipping a faux gin and tonic: sparkling water with a slice of lime.

Are you abusing alcohol? Try this test:

✓ Do you ever crave, not just desire, alcohol?

✓ At a party, do you often get drunk?

✓ Do you usually have more than one or two drinks in an evening?

✓ Do you ever drink before going to class?

✓ Have family or friends commented about how much alcohol you consume?

---

[7] Ibid.

If you answered yes to even one of these questions you probably have a drinking problem.[8] If you're concerned about alcohol or drug abuse, choose an alcohol- and drug-free dorm, or join a campus student group such as B.A.C.C.H.U.S. GAMMA or Students Against Drunk Driving (S.A.D.D.). If you already have a problem, join Alcoholics Anonymous (look in the phone book for a nearby location).

> **Tip: An easy way to say no is to volunteer to be the designated driver.**

With illegal drugs, you really should just say no. They are unregulated, so you can't be sure what they put into that pot: PCP, paraquat, all sorts of stuff that can toast your brain. And it has become clear that long-term use of marijuana will lower your brain power and motivation. Stronger drugs are like Russian roulette, but fortunately not many students are that foolish, so we won't talk about that poison here. In addition, they are illegal.

PARENTAL NOTE While this is a personal decision, in general, parents may be wise to take a moderate approach. If you insist on absolute abstinence from drinking, drugs, or sex, you increase the risk of your child rebelling once he's away from your watchful eye. However, if you wink at getting drunk or stoned, you also increase your child's likelihood of abuse. What often works best is a message that says something like, "Your decision to occasionally use alcohol or pot or not to is a personal one. If you decide not to, terrific. If you decide to do it, I would only ask that you consider being moderate, and to not drive while under the influence."

---

8 Jason Rich, *The Everything College Survival Book.* (Holbrook, MA: Adams Media, 1997).

CRITICAL DECISION #10:
AM I GOING TO SMOKE CIGARETTES?

Tobacco companies seduce millions of teenagers into smoking, even though the corporations know it will kill half of those teens, most of them to cancer, probably *the* most painful way to die. Do you really want to let that happen to you?

IMPORTANT! According to a government report, half of smokers who began when they were teenagers will eventually die from it, probably prematurely in middle age. That cuts 20 to 25 years from your life expectancy! Think about it, dying 20 to 25 years sooner? And for what? So you can turn off your friends because your breath and clothes stink? So you can enjoy the benefits of yellow teeth? So you can't taste food as well? So your babies have a greater chance of being born deformed? Oh, and let's not forget about the money. Smoke a pack a day and we're talking more than $1,000 each and every year! Can you think of anything you could spend $1,000 on that doesn't have the above liabilities?

Yeah, I can hear you say, "but smoking is cool." What would you say if your twin said she smoked because it was cool? Or because it calms her down? Or what if your twin said, "It's OK. I can stop whenever I want."

Are you already addicted? See if your college's health center offers smoke-enders groups. Or call 1-800-4-CANCER. Better to call them now for information on ways to stop smoking than to call them later to find out about chemotherapy to treat your cancer.

CRITICAL DECISION #11:
WHAT ACTIVITIES AM I
GOING TO GET INVOLVED IN?

A Carnegie Foundation study found that only 36 percent of college students participate in student activities other than sports. So, if you think you might like to get involved in a campus activity, get the list of your college's clubs, extracurricular activities, and organizations. It's usually in the catalog or in a booklet available at your college's student union or office of student activities.

> **When I show graduates a list of extracurriculars offered at their college, the most frequent response is, "Wow, I would have done that if I had known it was available."**

Because many students never see this list, some colleges run activities fairs at which representatives of dozens of student organizations sit at tables answering questions. Check out a few organizations and you'll probably find at least one that fits. And don't forget about campus bulletin boards and the student newspaper. They're more likely to clue you in on adventurous opportunities not listed in official college publications.

Get Mentored, Then Become a Mentor

Most campuses offer a junior or senior mentor to freshmen, especially to minorities. Mentoring is rewarding both for the mentor and the protege. There's nothing like a one-on-one relationship.

Clubs

Every college has dozens of student clubs, and if none suits you, most colleges will help you start your own.

INSIDER'S SECRET Leadership positions, which can help you prepare for later success, often go unfilled. For example, I heard that at St. Mary's College of Maryland, there was a frantic search for a yearbook editor just before work on it had to begin. On every campus, there are student organizations without a strong leader. These are opportunities just waiting to be taken. Students in these positions often get to participate in a campus leadership program that teaches them public speaking, how to effect change, and how to develop confidence—things that, in the long run, may help you more than most courses.

Clubs affiliated with your major are often more interesting than you might think. A biology majors' club might include a field trip to see gene therapy at a biotech company, a seminar on careers in genetics followed by a party, or a talk on bioethics followed by a softball game. These clubs give you the chance to meet students with a common interest. You find out the courses and professors to take and those to avoid. You get to meet dedicated professors on an informal basis, which can yield good advice, a mentor, and research opportunities. Many students find that joining a major-affiliated club even increases their interest in their major, which makes it easier to study.

Student Government

Student governments usually decide how to spend many thousands of dollars, and advise administration on everything from affirmative action to entertainment. You don't need to win an election to get involved. Student government has many committees that need members, even chairs. Many positions go vacant because students don't know about them. Leadership opportunities are also available in residence hall government.

Campuswide Committees

At many colleges, there are student members on the faculty senate, the president's roundtable, and so on. At Queens College (NY), students make up one-third of the academic senate. These committees plan student activities, establish campuswide policies, and select award winners. If you're interested, talk with someone in the office of student affairs.

Honors Program

As discussed on pp. 155–156, this often enables you to have an Ivy experience at a regular ol' college.

Service Organizations

These groups do good works such as helping the elderly or illiterate. Often members of a service organization get together for parties and other social events. Many campuses have a clearinghouse of community service opportunities. Others have a chapter of Alpha Phi Omega, a fraternity that emphasizes service.

State or Nationwide Professional Organizations

Such organizations exist for majors in most fields, for example, the American Psychological Association. They often have local chapters and annual state and national conventions, which allow you to rub elbows with active professionals and students in your field from around the nation. Grad schools like to see these on your application, especially if you presented a paper.

Student Newspaper

Here, you can hone your writing skills and hang out with some of the campus's more outspoken students. Working on the newspaper can also make you feel like you're making a difference.

Radio Station

From working as a DJ to doing promotions, campus radio station gigs are fun and may even pave the way to a future career. The news department is often a particularly interesting place to work.

Intercollegiate Sports

Even though I was a benchwarmer, I loved playing baseball in college. But if you're thinking that varsity play could be a ticket to the pros, remember that unless you're a high school All-American who will be a star on a NCAA Division I top-25 team, you have a better chance of being named president of the college.

Making Connections

Even if you're not particularly interested in making career-boosting connections, it's fun to see how the other half lives. Consider extracurriculars that tend to attract the wealthy and well-connected.

✓ golf, tennis, sailing, rugby, fencing, lacrosse, or crew teams

✓ fraternities or sororities

✓ formal dances on campus

✓ expensive on-campus housing

✓ expensive university-sponsored recreation

✓ the student arm of the alumni association. Many colleges encourage students to help alumni to plan activities such as homecoming and parents' weekend. If your school's alumni association doesn't have a student arm, see if students are allowed to join the regular alumni association.

<hr>

PARENTAL NOTE During the first week of college, ask if your child has looked into any extracurricular activities. If not, ask your child to consider visiting the student activities office to get the master list.

<hr>

CRITICAL DECISION #12:
SHOULD I GO GREEK?

At their best, fraternities and sororities offer a lot. They provide a built-in social life. They can offer lasting friendships and career connections. Greeks play an active role in campus social life and traditions such as homecoming. Many Greek organizations do considerable community service, for example, "adopting" home-bound senior citizens. Greek organizations also provide exceptional leadership opportunities within the house and in campuswide government, because Greek organizations often vote as a block. It's not unusual for half of the student government to be Greek, although fewer than 10 percent of the student body are members.

All these opportunities may explain why a *Fortune* magazine study found that 22 U.S. presidents and 17 vice-presidents, and more than 70 percent of the officers of the 750 largest United States corporations who went to colleges with Greek organizations belong to them. The majority of U.S. senators are Greeks, as are Ruth Bader-Ginsberg, Jesse Jackson, Georgia O'Keeffe, David Letterman, and Ted Koppel, to name a few.

> **Contrary to the stereotype, Greek organizations can even help your grades. Many houses have mandatory study hours, in-house study buddies, and old test files; and they boast grades at or above the campuswide average.**

Some fraternities and sororities are deemphasizing the role of alcohol, for example, by having dry rushes, and eschewing kegs in favor of bring-your-own-cans.

Unfortunately, many fraternities and sororities are not like this. Pledging can mean six months of slavery: "Hey, pledge, clean up after the party! I don't care about your econ final. You should have studied earlier, boy!"

Even after you're a member, some houses aren't overly concerned about coursework. Your grades won't be helped by living in a fraternity that schedules Cowboy Night during finals week. At some fraternities, the *typical* member drinks a gallon of beer in a night, at least once a week. And here is a statistic so shocking I can't even believe it: according to an Associated Press report that was cited in *Time* magazine, 86 percent of fraternity residents "are presumed to be binge drinkers."

Clearly, not all Greek-letter organizations are alike, so be a good shopper. Rush week is when you and the Greek organizations check each other out. Are they right for you? Are you right for them?

Some members, looking back after college graduation, felt that Greek life forced them to spend too much time on silly rituals and traditions, and caused them to interact primarily with look-alike/act-alike/think-alike people. And it can get expensive.

Before you get bombarded by the sales pitches during rush week, speak with an unbiased source: an officer on the Interfraternity or Panhellenic Council or the college sponsor. These people often have lots of information on each house (for example, grade point average, the number of complaints lodged against it, how much it raised for charity). They know which are *Animal Houses*, which require a designer wardrobe, and which subject pledges to harassment. Tom Dougan, Executive Officer of Student Affairs at the University of Rhode Island, said, "I love when students call about fraternities and sororities. I give them the straight scoop."

Hazing is the harassment and ridicule of pledges. University of Texas freshman Mark Seeberger was forced to consume 18 ounces of rum within two hours—giving him a blood alcohol content of .43. (A person is legally drunk at .05–.10.) Seeberger was then dropped off in a rural location and forced to find his way home. He never made it. This absurd practice now occurs only at some houses. Do you really want to join a fraternity or sorority in which your worth is determined by how much punishment you're willing to take?

Here are some more tips:

✓ Don't "suicide," that is, rush only one house. Its members may not be as crazy about you as you are about them.

✓ Don't rely on reputation. Tappa Nu Keg may have developed its good reputation based on the national fraternity, not the local, or on past years' members, not the current crop.

✓ Will you have to conform to a narrow set of values? College is supposed to broaden your perspective. Some Greek houses narrow it.

✓ Don't decide based on a party. Visit the house on a typical week-night and weekend day. Ask questions such as:

How is your fraternity or sorority different from others?
Describe your pledging process. What will you expect from me? What can I expect from your chapter?
After I'm a member, in a typical week, how much time will I be asked to devote to I Phelta Thi?
How much should I budget for a year in your fraternity or sorority?
How big a role does sports play in your fraternity? Charity work?

What's the worst thing you make pledges do?

What costs are involved in membership? What "extras" inevitably come up (for example, buying presents for big brothers/sisters, purchasing photos at the weekly dance, "must" ski trips)?

Sure, a few houses may reject you for asking these questions, but that's fine. You want a house where someone who asks intelligent questions is welcomed, not ridiculed. This may sound corny, but it's important: Be yourself when you rush. Phoniness may land you a bid, but once in, you'll have to keep up the act for four years or risk becoming an outcast. If a fraternity or sorority doesn't want the real you, you don't want it. There are many other social groups on campus, from choral clubs to karate clubs, that will accept you for who you are. On the other hand, if you are wondering why you were rejected from ten of ten fraternities, it may be valuable to ask for feedback.

CRITICAL DECISION #13:
SHOULD I SEEK OUT PROFESSORS?

You'll probably grow as much from your one-on-one relationships as from your classes. We've already talked about how to develop good one-on-one relationships with students. Here we'll talk about professors.

Your Advisor

You'll probably be assigned an advisor, usually a professor in your prospective major. My daughter had heard about a wonderful professor, Jennifer Wilson, and requested her as an advisor. That turned out to be key to her college experience.

If you're lucky, your advisor will not only know what courses you have to take, she'll recommend great profs, help you plan a program that gets you a good education without overloading your schedule, ensure that you don't find out three days before you expect to graduate that you're missing History 236b, help you plan your future, and ponder the meaning of life with you.

But let me be honest with you. Your chances of getting a great advisor are about as good as of swatting a fly with a hammer. At nearly every college I've reviewed, advising is the #2 student complaint. (Parking is #1.) Why is advising usually so lousy? At most colleges, the quality of advising doesn't count when faculty are being considered for salary increases. So, if your advisor sounds like *he* needs advising, request a switch from the secretary of your major department.

The Virtual Advisor

No matter how good your advisor, chances are there is important stuff that your advisor doesn't know. So consult the advisor that's guaranteed to be knowledgeable: the college catalog, in print or at the college's web site. It has most of what you need to know, is available 24 hours a day, seven days a week. Be sure to identify the courses you're required to take for graduation and for your major. That will help you get started early, and avoid ending up being a teary college senior who thinks she's going to graduate, only to find she's missing some course that won't be offered for the next three semesters.

Finding a Mentor

A mentor is more than an advisor. A mentor is a career and life coach. When you're applying to college, the idea of a mentor may sound good. Imagine a wise professor inviting you to coffee, you working at his or her elbow on an important research project, receiving door-opening letters of recommendation,[9] and finding a lifetime friend.

But once at college, these visions are often replaced by new ones, such as appearing stupid in front of a professor. These visions cause students to avoid professors.

Fortunately, these visions are distorted. The vision of the inaccessible professor is sometimes

Professors don't expect undergraduates to be wise. Frankly, they expect them to be passive. So, if you take the initiative and ask questions (anything but "Will this be on the midterm?"), they'll respect you more.

incorrect. Even at large colleges, many professors are open to meeting with motivated students. And those meetings rarely are medieval torture treatments. A study found that the most frequently discussed topics are answering student questions about the course, job prospects, money, and careers, followed by boy/girlfriends, lifestyles, movies, popular music, world problems, and social events. Not quite the academic grilling you might have feared. If you're nervous about having to answer a question on the spot, try e-mail.

After a couple of meetings with a professor whom you like, take a risk. Ask, "Might you need a student assistant? Or could I do an independent study (see p. 130) with you?"

---

[9] Half of students graduate from large colleges without knowing a single professor well enough to request a letter of recommendation.

The thought of working for a professor may be intimidating. How can "average you" work for a brilliant professor? Relax. You don't need to be a genius. She's got the genius. What she needs is someone earnest, reliable, and enjoyable to work with. That would be you.

Many students feel more comfortable getting advice and personal attention from someone other than a professor. That's okay. See a resident assistant in your dorm, a friendly classmate, an older student, a teaching assistant, someone in your major department's student organization, a member of the student honor society, someone who works in the office of student affairs, a campus chaplain, or someone from the college's student learning center.

CRITICAL DECISION #14:
WHAT CLASSES SHOULD I TAKE?
HOW MANY?

Top Five Rules for Choosing Courses

1. Unless you're a strong student, for the first term, take four courses rather than the usual five. Just getting used to college life is a course in itself. Take one course in your prospective major; one or two that fulfill requirements for graduation; and pick one simply because it sounds exciting.

2. Take mainly standard courses your first year, for example, Introduction to Biology, English Composition, Western Civilization. These courses usually meet graduation requirements no matter what your major, and if, by any chance, you decide to transfer, most colleges will award you credit for these courses.

3. Limit yourself to one or two killer courses per term. Most students find the following courses tough: chemistry, physics, calculus, literature (lots of reading).

    On most campuses, most students find these easier: introductory courses in psychology, education, sociology, women's studies, ethnic studies, physical education, music, and art.

4. Even large colleges offer some small classes. Try to take at least one per term, for example, a freshman seminar, a course in a living/learning program (see pp. 160–161), or an honors class. Often you can find one that will meet a graduation requirement. Small classes not only may teach you more, they're a source of friends—you're having discussions with a dozen students for 10 to 15 weeks, so there's bound to be someone you click with.

5. If your goal is to transfer, contact the college to which you want to transfer before registering for your first semester at your first college. Find out which courses the second college wants you to take. Get it in writing!

IMPORTANT! When in doubt, choose the teacher rather than the course title. European Linguistics taught by a great teacher is usually better than Human Sexuality taught by a dud.

Ways to Find Life-Transforming Professors

Ask at orientation.

Ask students.

Ask your advisor or other professor, especially one whose class you liked.

Consult the list of teaching award winners. It's usually at the college's web site, in the catalog or at the office of academic affairs.

Check student ratings of professors. At the end of most college courses, students fill out a form evaluating their instructors. At some colleges, students have access to the results. Check with the student government office.

Attend a meeting of the club for students majoring in your field. Ask who's good.

Ask the department secretary, teaching assistants, resident assistants, and other students.

Ask the department secretary for a copy of the syllabus. This describes the course and lists the required readings and assignments.

Look at the required books in the bookstore.

Talk with the professor about his or her upcoming course.

I love this one: Overenroll. If you're planning on taking five courses, enroll for six. Go to the first class meeting of all six, then drop the worst. No need to put up with a professor who speaks incomprehensible English or assigns five incomprehensible books.

Top Seven Rewarding Courses

1. **Courses in real-life survival skills.** Take a course in public speaking, a writing course, word processing/spreadsheets/databases, business, human sexuality, or the Internet.

   A special pitch for writing courses. They're usually taught in a small class in which you'll get valuable feedback on your writing. Write better and you'll do better in most of your other courses. As important, writing improves your thinking skills, and, you probably could use that—even if you got As in high school English. And if you're thinking, "Yuck, I hate writing," that's all the more reason to take it.

2. **Independent study** (also called a tutorial). A tutorial is not tutoring. It's a one-on-one course with your choice of professor on a topic of your choice that isn't covered in a regular course. It sounds scary, but it's usually much more interesting and custom-tailored than a regular course. How do you get a tutorial? Just ask a cool professor.

   > **Taking a few independent studies is one of the smartest things you can do at college.**

   Surprisingly, even at large colleges, he often will say yes. If so, you and the prof will jointly decide what you'll read, and then meet every week or two to grill you to uncover your every weakness. (Just kidding.) You'll usually write a paper or two and then receive course credit. It's a way to study what you want, with whom you want, in a class of one! Great letters of recommendation often result.

3. **Honors classes.** Typically, these are small classes with top students taught by the best professors. That's what I call a patch of Ivy.

4. Study abroad programs. In looking back, many college graduates said they grew most from studying abroad.

INSIDER'S SECRET Even if you don't plan on studying abroad until your junior year of college, start investigating now. Many top programs have very early deadlines.

5. Courses with discussion sections. In these, for two or three hours a week you sit listening to a lecture. Then for one hour a week, the large lecture is broken up into small discussion groups, usually led by a graduate student. This can be a nice blend; you get to hear the ideas of the brilliant professor yet enjoy the personal attention and more active learning that comes from a small class led by a graduate student.

6. New ideas classes. One of college's main purposes is to expose you to new ideas. If your politics are conservative, take a course on Marx. If you think government should aid the unfortunate, attend an Objectivist or Skeptics club meeting. You'll feel more secure in your viewpoint, be better able to defend your position to others or to yourself, or you might even change your views. College offers a unique opportunity to grow.

7. Cooperative Education. No, this doesn't mean you do each other's term papers. Co-op education refers to internships that earn college credit. (See p. 166 for information.)

Crashing a Class

You try to register for a class. The perhaps digitized voice says, "I'm sorry. Course closed." The savvy student, if he really wants the class, ignores the voice, runs to the professor's office before the first day of class, and asks to be added to the class roll: "I really want to take your class because [*insert amazing reason here*]." If the professor says no, the student responds, "Well might I just sit in? If, by any chance, enough students drop the course, maybe you'll allow me to enroll. And if worse comes to worst, even if I can't enroll, I will have learned the material." You'll usually get in.

CRITICAL DECISION #15:
HOW CAN I GET COURSE CREDIT
THE EASY WAY?

Advanced Placement

If you've scored at least 3 on an Advanced Placement exam, be sure your college transcript shows you've received credit for that course. Some colleges insist on a 4.

International Baccalaureate

Many colleges award credit for International Baccalaureate courses taken in high school. Check to be sure they've credited you.

CLEP

The same folks who bring you the SAT exams have another test. You may be happy to take this one. If you pass a 90-minute exam in any of dozens of subjects, most colleges will credit you with a full college course! Before starting to study for these exams, check with your college to make sure they'll give you credit. If so, for exam information call: 609-771-7865 or visit *www.collegeboard.com*.

Challenge a Course

Think you know enough about a subject to pass the final exam even if you haven't taken the course? Perhaps by studying the textbook? Or because of your life experience? If so, ask the professor of the course if you can "challenge" the course. Most professors will agree to give you the equivalent of a final exam. Pass and you get credit for the entire course!

Want a way to make a tough course easier? Take it during the summer. Classes are generally smaller, professors are in a better mood, and you only have that one monster course to concentrate on.

Are you a so-so student but would love to see what it's like to attend a designer-label college? Many—for example, Berkeley and Cornell—

are nearly open admission during the summer. But check with your advisor to be sure the course credit will transfer.

Distance Courses

Visit *www.petersons.com/distancelearning/code/search.asp* or get a copy of the *Independent Study Catalog* (Peterson's, revised periodically). They list thousands of online text-, audio-, or videotape-based courses that you can take in the comfort of your room, at your own pace, usually at a bargain price. Many colleges will accept these courses in place of their own, but check with your advisor to be sure. Beware: Many students who start a distance course never finish. These courses are terrific for the self-starter, a risk for the procrastinator.

CRITICAL DECISION #16: HOW AM I GOING TO LEARN SOMETHING IN THIS CLASS?

Most of us want to get good grades, acquire skills, and have time left for fun. That's what this section is all about—minimally painful ways to boost your grades and ensure you remember something of value long after the course is over.

Ways to Stay Awake and Learn Something

Read first. If you've done the assigned reading before rather than after class, you'll understand the lecture better, and so be more likely to stay awake. If it's a discussion class, you're more likely to participate, which also helps you stay awake. Most important: **show up.** Martin Spethman, author of *How to Get into and Graduate from College in Four Years,* points out the problem. "You skip class because you are behind, don't want to be called on, or the lecturer is boring. So you'll have to rely on the notes of someone who was there, which means they probably won't be clear to you. So, by next class, you'll be further behind. You can break the vicious cycle: Go to just one lecture prepared, change your seat, and sit next to someone cute to keep you wanting to come."

Sit in a power seat. Everyone knows it's easier to pay attention in the front seats, but there's more to it than that. Each instructor's eyes tend to focus on one area, for example, one-quarter of the way back and slightly to one side of center. These *power seats* are the places to be. From there, the instructor is more likely to see your eye contact and frequently raised hand. Besides, it's hard to chat, doodle, or read the college newspaper with the teacher's eyes beaming down at you every few seconds like searchlights. Power seats are the places to be, but I know some students who would rather sit anywhere than in a power seat, especially if it's a lousy prof. Ironically, that's when a power seat is most important.

Don't let a lousy prof mess you up. The kiss of death is to think; "I can't learn from this guy. I don't like him." Or "She has this terrible accent." Anyway, now you're stuck, so your reaction to a lousy teacher has to be, "I'll work twice as hard." It's easy to do well with a great teacher, but they're not that common because at most colleges, professors are hired and promoted more on how much research they do than on how well they teach. Good students learn how to avoid the worst professors and learn plenty from the average ones. Spethman advises, "Make them earn their money. Don't let them race through a lecture without explaining clearly anything you don't understand."

Get active. When you find yourself spacing out, listen hard for 10 to 20 seconds, then ask yourself; "What should I do: Take a note, say something, apply the professor's comment to my life, or do nothing?" Keep doing that and you'll stay awake, the time will go more quickly, and you'll learn more.

IMPORTANT! Asking a question or making a comment is a triple winner. It makes you learn more, you get personalized feedback, and you impress the teacher. As a former prof, I know that instructors appreciate all questions. Even a dumb question lets us know the student cares and gives us feedback on what was and wasn't clear. What we hate is indifference—bored faces and slouching bodies.

Rule of thumb: in discussion classes, speak up one to three times per hour.

What if you want to make a comment or ask a question in a supersized class? Write it in the margin and speak to the professor after class, during the discussion section, or during the prof's office hours.

Take a Moderate Amount of Notes

The lecture. You're going to have to endure lots of these often boring one-way communications. Unfortunately, you'll also be tested on them. That means take good notes or die.

Even if it's important, don't write something you already know. Because you're not writing so much, you have time to think about what the instructor is saying. You'll leave class having already understood much of the material and with a manageable amount of notes to review. Rmbr. Take a mod amt of notes. Ok?

The best note takers write fairly little, jotting down only the phrases (never whole sentences) that summarize the main points they do not already know.

How do you know what you can skip? Consider taking a note when the instructor seems to be emphasizing a point. How can you tell? Tip-offs include when he slows the rate of speech, repeats himself, writes on the board, uses hand gestures, speaks louder, spends a lot of time on one point, or uses phrases that let you know he's saying something important: "The main point is," "Therefore," "To summarize," "Let me make this clear," or the subtle, "On the test I might ask..."

If you wonder whether your notes are any good, show them to your prof. If she rolls on the floor laughing, listen up and try again.

Don't cram. Good note takers lock in their learning by rereading and maybe even reorganizing their notes that day, to make sure they're in good

Handouts from the professor are likely to find their way onto tests. Attach them to your notes.

enough shape to be useful in studying for the test. It can be helpful and fun to do it with a smart classmate. You may be able to fill in what the partner missed.

If something in your notes is unclear, make a note to ask about it the next day. A day or two before the test, good note takers usually only need to do a brief general review and then focus on any weak spots. No cramming and probably a good test score.

At the end of the course, I know it's tempting to throw away your notes, but consider saving them—they might help in another course, and at minimum, they'll have nostalgia value. I guarantee that 20 years from now, you'll be amazed to see how much you've forgotten.

CRITICAL DECISION #17: PREPPING FOR TESTS

Ways to Get an A and Remember Something Afterward (Even if You're Not a Genius)

Study after each class: Revise your notes and read the chapter. Cramming is the kiss of death. Even if, after cramming, you do well on the test (doubtful), you'll forget most of it two seconds after the test. So, you'll have wasted all that time and tuition just to have a good time. You can do that at home for free.

It's often tough to study in your dorm. Use these sources of peace and quiet: a quiet room in the residence hall or the library (not the room in which everyone's flirting); outdoors under a tree; chapel; tutoring center; park bench; in your car; an empty classroom; a coffeehouse with booths so you can stretch out.

Ever finish reading an assignment and wonder what it was about? Here's a surefire preventive. As you read, follow each line down with your hand. This helps you stay focused and keeps you from losing your place. **Read only a paragraph or two, then turn away and recite what you remember.** If you've left out something important, say it aloud and, in the margin, bracket that part so you can reread it just before the test.

Or even easier, when you feel yourself spacing out, read the important stuff aloud. It's hard to space out while reading aloud. Also you'll remember it better because you're going slowly and because you're hearing your voice at the same time as you're seeing the words.

If you don't understand a section, reread it only once. If you still don't understand it, just mark it with a question mark, and go on. Staying stuck is very frustrating. At the end of the chapter, call a friend or ask the instructor about your question marks. This approach to reading also works well when studying your class notes.

Write a response. After reading a section, write whatever you want about it. For example; what made you angry, happy, or confused about what you read? What do you most want to remember? Is any of it relevant to your life?

Pace the floor while studying hard stuff. Walking increases the circulation to the brain.

Use different highlighters for different stuff. Try hot pink for the stuff most likely to be on the exam and yellow for other stuff worth highlighting. Not only does this keep you awake, the color is a memory jogger.

Ask the instructor what to focus on in studying for a test. You'll likely get more help by asking during an office hour. "Any suggestions as to the wisest approach to studying for the exam?"

For memorization tests, make flash cards at least a week in advance. If you make them up last-minute, you'll spend most of your time making and little memorizing.

Meet regularly with one, two, or three study partners. Take turns asking your partners questions you think could be on the test. But one U.S.C. student warned, "Between the fool-around time and the time helping a girl who didn't prepare for the study group, I would have learned more if I studied by myself. I did have a good time, though." Moral of the story: Choose your study partners carefully.

Create a pretend crib sheet. Imagine the instructor allowed you to bring one sheet of paper of notes into the exam. What would you write (small handwriting permitted)? On the night before the exam, just study that sheet.

Avoid guilt. A student once asked me, "I've heard that no matter how much you study, you can't read everything that's required. Is that true?" I met with the Student Honor Society at Berkeley, some of the best students at the nation's most prestigious public university. Every one of these superstudents agreed that it's impossible to read everything that is required, let alone recommended. Some profs give assignments as though their course is the only one you're taking. Here are a few ways to deal with the problem of too much to read.

✓ *Read what you like.* Some students personalize their education by devoting most effort to what they're interested in. They do enough work on their other subjects to get acceptable grades, but save the extra effort for the courses they're most interested in.

✓ *Flexible reading.* Read the way you drive a car. There are times to read at 60 mph, other times at 30, and when you get to hard but important concepts, it's stop-and-go.

✓ *Skim the book.* Supplement with *Cliff's Notes* or *Barron's Book Notes*. This may be the only option if the professor expects you to read *Ulysses* in one week. *Cliff's* or *Barron's Book Notes* provide a plot summary and analysis of themes, characters, and symbolism.

Top Five Keys to Successful Test Taking

5. Have you ever written four essays and found out later that the instructions said, "Choose three of four"? The easiest way to boost your test score is to read the directions and questions carefully. If you're not sure of what's being asked, don't be afraid to ask the instructor.

4. The most important test-taking skill? Knowing how to conquer the tough questions. Even A students encounter items they're unsure of, but instead of getting flustered and making a wild guess, they spend some extra seconds figuring out a way to make an intelligent one.

3. When I was in the seventh grade, our science teacher told us that on a multiple-choice test, when you're absolutely stuck between two choices, choose the one that's closest to the middle because test makers tend to hide the correct answer in the middle. I'm not sure he's right, but I always followed his advice whenever two choices looked equally good. It just felt better to have some way of choosing.

2. On essay tests, first read all the questions, then begin with the easiest one and work your way up. This way, if you don't have time

to finish, the hardest essays will be left undone. Also, doing easier essays builds confidence and may even trigger thoughts on the hard ones.

1. You get the test back. Don't do what I did when I was in college, which was look at the grade, quickly scan the red marks, and stuff the test into my notebook. Look carefully at those red marks. They are individualized feedback, the stuff that private colleges charge big bucks for.

INSIDER'S SECRET Think of the returned test paper as a study plan for the next exam. The College Board says, "Virtually all students study *for* tests. Good students study *from* tests," especially the wrong answers. Look at each error you made. What can you learn from that error, both for your learning and as a clue to how to do better on the next test? Then look at the test as a whole. Did the exam focus on big concepts or trivial facts? On material from class or from the text? The next test will likely be similar.

CRITICAL DECISION #18:
I'VE GOT THIS PAPER TO WRITE

Even if you get A's on your papers, your writing could probably use improvement. Because most teachers want their best students to get into prestigious colleges, they think they should give A's to the top 10 to 30 percent of each class's papers, even if they're not very good.

Whether or not you get A's, it's important to learn to write well because you'll always need to write, everything from work memos to love letters.

If at all possible, pick a topic you're excited about. Many instructors will let you write on a topic other than the assigned one.

Here's my approach to writing. It's worked pretty well: I've had four critically and commercially successful books and more than 400 articles published.

Occasionally, I start by making a brief outline, but usually, I jump right in. In my first draft, I have low standards: I write whatever decent idea pops into my head.

Often, having written that first sentence, I immediately see a way to improve it. If so, I make the change. If not, I move

It's much easier to revise your way into excellence than to come up with perfection out of thin air.

on to the next sentence. I repeat that process until I've finished the first draft. I do not get out of my chair until that draft is done.

INSIDER'S SECRET Usually, hard-to-understand writing is caused by not taking the time to figure out how to say it simply, or by trying to impress with big words or long sentences. If you find yourself having written a complicated sentence or paragraph, turn away from what you've written and say the thought in your own words. That will often be a clearer way to say what you're trying to say.

Your writing will also be boring if you include nonessential details. In writing each sentence, ask yourself, "is this detail important enough to risk boring the reader?' Every nonessential detail dilutes your paragraph.

What if an instructor says, "I want a ten-page paper"? It's tempting to pad; to include nonessential details and use many words to express a simple idea, but your report will be worse. The solution is to come up with more ideas. Don't have any? Try the Internet or library, or ask someone you respect.

After finishing a first draft, I revise and revise it until I'm pleased with it. I typically reread a draft four to eight times. I stop only when a reread doesn't improve it anymore. I then put it aside for a day and review it with fresh eyes. Almost always, I find yet additional ways to improve it. The result is usually a work I feel good about, and one that gets published.

HELP!

Worthington and Farrar warn that you will run into problems at college. It's inevitable. But they also point out the good news, that "college is one of the few situations in life in which hundreds of people exist simply to help you find your way. Counselors, tutors, faculty and resident assistants, financial aid people, health care workers, librarians, campus security, members of the clergy—they're all there for you. If you're hesitant to use their services, remember that your tuition helps pay for their presence. Not using these services is like driving up to the gas pump, paying for $10 worth and driving off after getting just $5 worth."[10] Also remember that it's no shame to use these services. Even many top students use them.

The most important thing is to do something *now*. Don't hold off until finals when it's too late. Take an honest look at yourself and figure out why you're doing badly. If it's an emotional problem, see a campus counselor. If you're not understanding the material, get a tutor. If your professor hates your papers, see him or her. If you're not spending enough time studying, reserve more study time each week, as rigidly scheduled as if it were an additional class. If a class is miles over your head, consider dropping it.

CRITICAL DECISION #19: "I JUST DON'T GET IT."

"Of course it's hard. It's supposed to be hard. If it wasn't hard, everyone would do it. It's the hard that makes it great."
Tom Hanks, the manager in A League of Their Own

Whether it's reading, writing, math, time management, study skills, or test anxiety, academic problems are more common than rice in China. Fortunately, there's help available on any campus. Don't let pride keep you from getting extra help if you need it.

Six Lines of Defense Against an Academic Problem

1. If you found a class session difficult (and that can be the very first session), **be sure you did the basics:** Did you read the material before class, concentrate hard in class, and review your class notes immediately after class? If not, try those things before doing anything else. If that doesn't work, proceed to step 2.

[10] Worthington and Farrar, *Ultimate College Survival Guide.*

2. Before the next class, **see the professor or teaching assistant.** They're usually impressed that you cared enough to seek help. Come in with specific questions you want help with. "I didn't understand the lecture" is not specific.

3. **A one-on-one tutor is the most potent way to improve.**

INSIDER'S SECRET And often the best and least expensive tutor is a student in your class. She's been attending your class sessions, reading your course readings, and solidifies her own knowledge by teaching it to you.

Student tutors are a bargain—you may only need to pay $10 to $15 an hour, perhaps for only a few hours. Just go up to a student who appears to know the material and seems like a patient person. Explain that you need a tutor. If you can't find someone in your class, ask your professor or the department secretary for a recommendation.

4. **Go to the campus' tutoring center.**

5. **If it's going to require too much effort to survive a class, drop it,** but be sure you use the extra time on the remaining classes, not watching TV.

6. **If necessary, switch to an easier major**—even if your parents would love you to be a doctor. Tell them that if you don't switch, you're going to need a doctor.

CRITICAL DECISION #20: "I'M UNHAPPY."

Top Ten Ways to Get Happier

10. Ask yourself, **"What has worked in the past to solve the problem?** Can I use that solution now?"

9. Ask yourself, **"What would my best self do to solve my problem?"** "What would my role model do?"

8. Talk into a mirror. **Pretend you were giving advice to your twin** who was feeling exactly as you are.

7. **Take your mind off your worries by immersing yourself in something constructive.** Get to work or help someone else. If you get a bad test score, go and study for an hour. If you just had a fight with a friend, go jogging.

   A variant on that is to choose a very ambitious goal, for example, deciding that you're going to be the next editor-in-chief of the student newspaper. Soon you might find yourself saying, "I don't have time to feel sorry for myself."

   The more you do, the more you'll feel you can do. The less you do, the less you'll feel you can do.

6. **If you need self-pity time, give yourself a finite amount.** Say, for example, "At 4:00, I'm going to make an appointment with a tutor."

5. **Fake it 'til you make it.** If you're feeling anxious, pretend you're carefree. It's amazing, but after a while, you may forget that you were pretending.

4. **Talk with your parents or a wise friend.**

3. **Start a peer support group.** Ask a few friends if they'd like to get together for a Thank God It's Friday session. If the first session goes well, schedule another.

2. **See an on-campus counselor.** Many students think that counseling is only for the screwed up. Not true. At some time, all of us have felt depressed, lonely, inadequate, unmotivated, indecisive, socially inept, test phobic, self-destructive, or aimless. Most colleges offer free group and individual counseling, and workshops on these as well as concerns such as time management, drugs/alcohol, eating disorders, insomnia, sexuality, choosing a major or career, and stress reduction.

   An emotional problem that has lasted for years is often a physical problem that can be helped with medication. See a doctor.

Some students worry that if they see a campus counselor, their parents might find out their deep dark secrets. Don't worry.

> **An emotional problem that has lasted for years is often a physical problem that can be helped with medication. See a doctor.**

Under almost all circumstances, the college cannot legally release information to your parents without your permission.

1. **Do something about your problem. If it doesn't work, try something else.** The key to getting unstuck is trying things. Even if an approach doesn't work, you're better off than you are now. Each time you try an unsuccessful approach, you're a step closer to finding a successful one. So try something, even a simple thing like buying yourself a present to cheer you up. Trying nothing is the one approach that practically ensures you'll stay stuck.

Eating Disorders

This problem deserves its own category because it's become epidemic: more than one million boys and at least five million girls suffer from an eating disorder. Do you insist you should weigh less than the height/weight charts say? Have you binged and then purged (vomiting, laxatives, or overexercise?) You may well have an eating disorder. The web site *www.nationaleatingdisorders.org* offers a lot of information to help you decide if you have a problem, plus a nationwide list of treatment providers and support groups. In addition, difficult though it may be, I'd urge you to discuss the issue openly with your parent(s).

CRITICAL DECISION #21:
AM I GOING TO TAKE WHATEVER COMES OR AM I GOING TO MAKE SURE I GET A FAIR DEAL?

If something is wrong with your college life, you or someone on campus can probably fix it.

Don't just accept a miserable roommate, weekends with nothing to do, a noisy room, a bad schedule, or a professor you can't understand.

A freshman at the University of Alabama scored 1300 on the SAT but wasn't smart enough to ask

A member of the orientation committee at Harvard gives the following advice to incoming students. If you think of this every time a problem arises, you'll be on the path to college heaven. She advises, "Fix it. If you can't, ask. If someone says no, ask someone else."

for a roommate when she was given a single room. She suffered in loneliness for an entire semester, when undoubtedly there were hundreds of women who would have loved to trade for her single.

CRITICAL DECISION #22:
SHOULD I TRANSFER?

At some point, many college students wonder if they should transfer to another college. Often their problems would transfer along with them, for example, under-preparedness for college-level work or poor social skills. These students should look inward for solutions.

Other students think about transferring the first time they cry. Give it at least a full semester before seriously considering a change. Might any of these help? Try a new roommate, a lighter or heavier courseload, more carefully picking professors, participating in an extracurricular activity, reaching out to make friends. Certainly, before tackling the huge hassle of transferring, talk with people you trust— wise friends, parents, siblings, your resident assistant or advisor.

One more way to avoid the pain of transferring is to try a semester at a campus with which your college offers exchange privileges. (See your college's web site.)

If you think you might want to transfer, be sure you're taking courses that your new college will accept. The safest choices are standard introductory college-level courses, for example, introduction to chemistry, psychology, political science, sociology, American literature, European history, calculus, and a foreign language.

Apply to a number of colleges. One may give you credit for all the courses you've taken, while another may not count half of them. To maximize your chances, submit catalog copy and even syllabi for courses you've taken. If you need housing, be sure the colleges you're considering offer housing to transfer students.

It may be difficult to keep your grades up if you're unhappy at a college, but with low grades, fewer colleges will be willing to take a chance on you.

Remember!

1. Carefully choose where you're going to live. All dorms are not alike. The dorms that may sound boring (for example, the honors or technology dorm) are often the best. (Why? See p. 101.)

2. Set ground rules with your roommate (see p. 111) and keep them.

3. Know how to manage your time and conquer procrastination. Although you'll probably hate this, the key to getting a lot done may be to get to bed early and get up early. The second key is having (and using) a daily to-do list.

4. The most potent method of overcoming procrastination is—no matter how yucky it feels—to force yourself to sit down and get started. Once you've started, you'll probably continue. Struggle with a stumbling block for just a minute or two. If you're still stuck, get help.

5. Growth takes place one-on-one. The key to a good college experience is relationships with your roommate, friends, advisor, professor. If you're not happy with the ones you have, get new ones. Make a point of finding one or more wonderful professors who are willing to be your mentors.

6. If you choose to drink alcohol, limit yourself to one or two drinks in an evening. If you drink more than that on a regular basis, you are in danger of becoming a permanent loser. Get help or get ready to ruin your life.

7. Take classes from the best professors. How to find them? Ask other students or the department secretary, consult the list of teaching award winners that is available from the office of academic affairs, and the student ratings of professors (if available). Overenroll—if you want five courses, sign up for six. Attend the first class of all six and drop the worst one.

8. Learn survival skills: become a good writer and public speaker. Learn how to use the Internet efficiently.

9. Show up for class and sit in a power seat: the seats where that professor focuses his eyes most of the time. As Woody Allen says, "80 percent of success is showing up."

10. Be an active learner. Students who make comments and ask questions learn more. Even if your question is dumb, the professor and non-jerk students will appreciate your asking. It may be the question they were too self-conscious to ask.

11. Get a sub-notebook computer—great for taking notes in class, doing research in the library, and writing your paper under a tree. Make sure it doesn't get ripped off.

12. Don't cheat. Even if you don't get caught, after you graduate you'll feel like an imposter. And cutting corners becomes more and more of a habit, which increases your chances of getting caught or feeling like an imposter. As a cheater, you'll know less. Like your sixth grade teacher always said, "You're only hurting yourself."

13. When there's a problem, don't let it slide. It will only get worse. Try to fix it. If you can't, ask someone. If they can't help, ask someone else. Not using campus support services when you need them is like driving into a gas station, paying $10 and driving off with only $5 worth of gas.

14. If you're struggling in class, consider hiring a classmate as a tutor.

15. Don't be afraid to fail. If you always hit the target, you're probably standing too close. When I was a grad student at Berkeley, I wasted a great opportunity. I had small classes taught by smart professors who were willing to give me as much time as I needed. But I was so afraid of appearing dumb that I never asked a question that might possibly reveal my ignorance, and I never took on a really challenging project. Yes, I got my degree, but I got only half as much out of it as I could have.

Appendix A

Want Help Figuring Out What You Want in a College?

DECISION 1: Do I want to consider two-year colleges? Four-year colleges? Both?

Top Ten Reasons to Consider Starting at a Two-year College (even if you're a good student)

Put a checkmark next to each reason that is important to you. See if your parents mark what you mark.

10. Good teachers.

SURPRISE: Teachers are often better at two-year colleges. Why? Because they're hired and promoted on how well they teach, not on how much research they crank out.

9. On average, classes are smaller.

8. You'll probably learn as much.

Probably because of #10 and #9 above, research indicates that students at two-year colleges learn as much as they would have in two years at a four-year college.

7. It's often easy to transfer from a two-year to a good four-year college.

Good grades at a two-year college and recommendations from your instructors can help wipe out a bad high school record. After two years of saving money and getting what can be a better-than-brand-name education, you may be able to transfer to a harder-to-get-into four-year college that would not have admitted you as a freshman. Bonus: your bachelor's diploma from a four-year brand-name college will look the same as if you had started there as a freshman.

6. It's a bargain.

Tuition at the average two-year college is half that of the average four-year public, and just 10 percent of the average four-year private college! Not only will most two-year colleges save your parents big bucks, you're more likely to graduate without loans to pay back, and you can save up for a cool place to live, that set of wheels, or more school.

5. You'd do better with less pressure.

Even some good students do better starting out in the more relaxed academic environment of a two-year college. At many two-year colleges, there are classes that attract top students—honors classes or courses like physics, philosophy, calculus, and poetry. Myth: Two-year colleges are only for dummies. There are some fine students at two-year colleges and some dim bulbs at four-year institutions.

4. It's a place where weak students are more likely to succeed.

College work is usually harder than high school. If your high school grade point average in academic subjects is less than 2.7 (below B– or 80) and your SAT score is below 900 on the old SAT, 1350 on the new SAT (ACT below 19), your chances of succeeding at a four-year college are poor. Fewer than 20 percent of such students graduate even when given five years. In other words, if five such students start college, only one will get a diploma. And importantly, even if you squeak by, you may well end up competing for jobs requiring college-level academic skills, which are not your strength. Two-year colleges offer lots of classes and out-of-class support designed for students who are weak in reading, writing, or math.

And know this. Two-year colleges offer courses to prepare you for many good careers that don't require a four-year degree, for example, telecommunications engineering technology, food preparation (chef), robotics, aircraft repair, and respiratory therapy (the people who take care of the victims of cigarette smoking).

3. There are many housing choices.

Some students are better off with another year or two at home. Besides, the *Animal House*-type fun in a dorm is only fun for so long—it's frustrating trying to crank out that paper while your hall-mates are cranking tunes. And how do you feel about sharing a bathroom with two dozen people—including members of the opposite sex?

If you do want to live in a dorm, a small percentage of two-year colleges do have dorms. If you decide to live in an apartment, you usually get your own room instead of being stuffed two or even three to a closet-sized dorm. And you get to choose your roommate.

2. You can usually go part time or at night, as well as during the day.

So it's easy to have a job while at a two-year college.

1. They're easy to get into.

As good as two-year colleges are, you'd think they'd be tough to get into, but most are 98.6 schools—virtually all you need to get in is normal body temperature. Most two-year colleges are open to all high school graduates, and the application usually doesn't require the SAT, ACT, or an essay.

Top Six Reasons to Consider Starting at a Four-year College

6. You want mainly A and B students in your classes.

You're the sort of student who will learn more if your classmates are good students. You suspect that at a two-year college, the many low achievers might tempt you to goof off. Many four-year colleges also have lots of weak students, but the small percentage of colleges that are filled with top students are almost all four-year colleges.

5. You want a college with a rich intellectual and cultural life.

Four-year colleges are more likely to have a large library, many guest speakers, clubs, well-attended football and basketball games, political demonstrations, and big-name concerts. Of course, not all four-year colleges are like this.

4. You want a strong sense of campus community.

At four-year colleges, many students are involved in on-campus sports, clubs, the student newspaper, orchestra, and so on. In contrast, many two-year colleges (although not most private two-year colleges) are grab-and-go schools—many students just grab their classes and go home.

3. **You want to attend a college at which many students live on campus.**

Four-year colleges are more likely to offer on-campus housing. Living on campus makes it easier to get to know other students and to have those late-night discussions about the meaning of life.

2. **You deeply want to attend a brand-name college.**

Even though you know you could start out at a two-year college and then finish up at a more prestigious four-year college, you'd feel very sad that you were starting off at a two-year college.

1. **It's easier to stay focused on schoolwork.**

At most two-year colleges, you can go to class at night or part time, which enables you to take a job, even full time. So many two-year college students are tempted to put most of their energy into their job.

Now, in light of what you've read, what's best for you? Circle "two-year," "four-year," or both on your *What I Want* list on p. 6. Before deciding, you might discuss it with your parent or a counselor.

Here comes a very important but confusing part. Stay with me. I'll try to make it as simple as I can.

DECISION 2: Do I want a college with:

- ✓ mainly A students (with 1250–1600 on old SAT, 1900–2400 on new SAT, or 28–36 on ACT)

- ✓ mainly B to A students (with 1050–1250 on old SAT, 1600–1900 on new SAT, or 22–27 on ACT)

- ✓ an honors program and mainly B students

- ✓ mainly B– to C students (with 900–1100 on old SAT, 1350–1650 on new SAT, or 18–21 on ACT)

If you're a B to A student, you'll probably be happiest at a college with mainly B to A students. But maybe not. (See, I told you it gets confusing.)

Top Five Reasons to Drop Down One Category

Put a checkmark next to any of these reasons that are important to you. See if your parents mark what you marked.

5. You'll be one of the better students at that college.

That usually means more personal attention from the professors. Imagine how you'd feel if a professor called you over after class, complimented you on your good work, and invited you to help on a research project. Picture what it would be like to have professors eager to help you get a good job or get into top graduate schools. (Yes, top students from easy-to-get-into colleges do get into top graduate schools.)

4. You're less likely to burn out.

The second most common complaint at the Student Health Service at Harvard is stress and burnout. At a less competitive college, you're less likely to burn out. Just as important, you'll have more time to get involved in out-of-class activities. Most college graduates feel they learned more outside the classroom than in. Amy, an A student in high school, attended a college with many B students. She had the time to be a peer health counselor on campus, a volunteer with pregnant teens in East L.A., managing editor of the feminist newspaper, and student and later teacher of a women's self-defense class. By the way, she graduated with a 3.9 G.P.A. and got into an Ivy League graduate school.

3. Because you're not routinely being stretched to the max, you can risk trying a challenging course.

Organic chemistry, anyone? You might even have time for a snowboarding trip or two.

2. You'll probably graduate with better self-esteem.

It feels great to be a star student. You'll tend to forget that your peers weren't all Einsteins.

1. Many of my happiest clients (and my daughter) attended a one-category-down college.

Top Six Reasons to Jump Up One Category

6. **Classes tend to be more challenging, so if you can keep up you'll learn more.**

   Are you the sort who would feel, "Hey, I'm in the big time. Sure it's hard but it's worth working hard to keep up."?

5. **Outside-of-class discussions tend to be more stimulating.**

   You'll find a few more ideas, a little less gossip. Again, you'll learn more. Are you the sort who would appreciate listening to all those smart people even if your comments aren't always the best?

4. **The atmosphere in on-campus housing may be more interesting.**

   It may be less centered on getting drunk, listening to loud music, and watching soap operas. Most students won't plan their schedules around reality TV. Are you the sort who would appreciate arguing with friends until 2 A.M. about affirmative action, the benefits of development versus environmental protection, or how to land a cool career?

3. **Extracurricular activities such as the student newspaper and drama productions are generally of higher quality.**

   That can make you happier at college. One tiny example: it's nice, every day, to have the option of reading a student-written newspaper filled with thoughtful discussions about everything from sex to George W. Bush, from J. Lo to what's right and wrong with the college.

2. **You're a late bloomer, and know you'll do better in college than your high school grades and test scores suggest.**

1. **Employers and graduate schools will be more impressed.**

   This advantage may not be as big as it seems. Will you get lower grades at a college with better students? Would you get worse recommendations from professors than if you were the big fish in the less selective pond? If so, the career advantage of a harder-to-get-into college may vanish. Imagine that you were a boss and had two job candidates, one with A grades and great letters of recommendation from a moderately selective college and another with B grades and lukewarm recommendations from a highly selective college. Are you sure who you'd choose?

One Reason Not to Jump Up a Category

Bill Mayher, author of *The College Mystique*, warns, "Research shows that some of the least successful college students have been the ones who barely squeaked into the college of their choice and then spent far too much of their academic careers wondering if they had the right stuff to be there." James Wickenden, former director of Harvard's Office for Graduate and Career Plans, says of the premed students he worked with who didn't get into medical school, "Had those students gone to other, less competitive colleges . . . they might have realized their career goals."[1]

An Interesting Alternative for Top Students: An Honors Program at a College with Mainly B Students

Denver college counselor Steve Antonoff said, "Many students mistakenly think honors programs are filled with geeks walking around for four years in caps and gowns." In reality, they're not much different from other students except that they're brighter and more motivated.

In an honors program, you typically get to take one course each term in a small class with top students taught by one of the college's best professors; in other words, a patch of Ivy at a regular ol' college. Many honors programs extend the Ivy experience outside the classroom by offering an honors dorm and special extracurricular activities, for example, getting to have a small group discussion with celebrities when they come to give a lecture on campus. But most of your classes and extracurricular life can be with "regular" students. That can be a nice balance. The honors designation on the diploma can open doors to top careers or graduate school. Two financial bonuses: Most of the best honors programs are at public universities, which are less expensive than private colleges. Also, honors students often get tuition discounts.

Institutions known for their high-quality honors programs are: College of William and Mary; Penn State; The Citadel; the Universities of California-Davis, California-Irvine, Delaware, Maryland, College Park; Massachusetts-Amherst; New Mexico; Oklahoma State; Oregon;

---

[1] Patrick, M. "N is for Saying No to the Ivy League," *Journal of College Admission,* Summer, 1998, pp. 3–5.

South Carolina; South Dakota; Texas; Utah; Washington; Wisconsin, Madison, Wisconsin, Eau Claire; Valencia Community College (a two-year college in Florida) This list was derived from the author's experience and an interview with Joan Digby, author of *Peterson's Honors Programs and Colleges* and senior official with the National Collegiate Honors Council. You can quickly assess the quality of any college's honors program using the approach on page 19.

If you want to shoot for a college that is one category higher

Can you be admitted to a college that is one category higher? It's easiest if:

✓ you're good enough to play for that college's varsity;

✓ you're Black, Hispanic, or Native American;

✓ your parent has donated big bucks to the college, especially if the library is named after him or her.

Your application will also get a boost if you're:

✓ from a small town far away from the college (colleges like students with unusual perspectives).

✓ applying to a college at which less than 45 percent of the students are of your sex. For example, women get an advantage at engineering colleges; men get a boost at former women's colleges such as Vassar, Mary Washington, Goucher, and Sarah Lawrence.

✓ the best musician, actor, or artist in your school. (No, an extraordinary talent for doing chalk drawings with your toes doesn't count.)

✓ a student leader at a regional or national level.

Even if you're none of the above, a strong application can sometimes do the trick. (Chapter 4, which begins on p. 43, shows you how to create one.)

Now, in light of what you've read, what's best for you? Circle "Mainly A," "Mainly B to A," or "Honors program at a college with mainly B students," or "Mainly B– to C+," on your *What I Want* list on p. 6. Before deciding, you might discuss it with your parent or counselor.

DECISION 3: How much am I willing to pay for college?

Most colleges won't put it to you this directly, but it's the truth. If your family's income is $60,000 to $130,000, over your four college years, you and your parents will probably have to cough up $40,000 to $120,000 *in cash*[2] (depending on the college's sticker price). In addition, you will need to take on $15,000 to $40,000 in loans, plus you may have to hold a part-time job during each of your college years. Remember—and this is very important to most families—if you take more than four years to graduate (and many students do!), you may get limited financial aid for year five. Prospects are even worse for year six and beyond.

There is little evidence that a more expensive education results in more learning or better job prospects, so if your family earns $60,000 or more, you might first consider low- or mid-priced colleges even if you want a small college. There are some good small public colleges, two-year and four-year.

It can be especially tempting to consider designer-label private colleges like Yale or Stanford. But the cost/benefit of attending even these schools is unclear. In their favor, you get to spend four years around the nation's brightest and most motivated students. These colleges tend to have high-quality facilities such as large libraries. They attract famous guest speakers and performers. Plus, you get the good feeling (and the career advantage) of being able to say you attended a designer-label college. On the other hand, almost 40 percent of 4,000 students surveyed at the nation's most prestigious colleges felt their college wasn't a good value.[3] If your family can easily afford the sticker price or you get at least $15,000 per year in cash financial aid, these colleges may be worth it. If not, think twice. See pp. xiii–xvi for my reasoning.

---

[2] You may get additional financial aid if you're
  a. an A student applying to a college with mainly B students.
  b. a star athlete.
  c. African American, Hispanic, or Native American, especially if your high school record is at least average for that college.

[3] Greene, Howard. *The Select: Realities of Life and Learning in America's Elite Colleges.* HarperCollins, 1998.

Definitely think twice before shelling out big bucks for large not-so-prestigious private colleges. Unless such a college gives you a big cash discount, you may be able to find a similar education at a public university for (over four years) $50,000 to $100,000 less.

Now, in light of what you've read, what's best for you? Turn to your *What I Want* list and write the maximum four-year sticker price you're willing to consider. A four-year total published price for an in-state public college, including a fair estimate for living expenses, is $50,000–$80,000; for a brand-name private, $130,000–$180,000. Before deciding, you might discuss it with your parent or counselor.

DECISION 4: What size college do I want?

Top 13 Reasons to Prefer Small Colleges (under 5,000 undergrads)

Put a checkmark next to any reasons that are important to you.

13. **Small colleges often pay more attention to students' application** essays, extracurriculars, and letters of recommendation. This may be important if your grades and test scores aren't so hot.

12. **Small colleges may feel less intimidating.** Within a few days, you will know where most things are on campus.

11. **Small colleges are better for students who might not have the self-discipline** needed to thrive amid the anonymity of a large college.

10. **You'll know most students.** Some students like the idea that when they walk across campus, they'll run into lots of people they know, which is fine unless you're having a bad hair day.

9. **Typical class size will be 20 to 25 rather than 100+.** This makes some students more likely to go to class, pay attention, participate, and do the work.

8. **Classes are taught mainly by professors,** and rarely by less well-trained graduate students.

7. **Much class time is spent listening to what your classmates have to say.** However, some college students end up considering this a disadvantage.

6. **Students, on average, are more serious about learning.**

5. **You'll do more writing assignments and take fewer multiple-choice tests.** Sure, multiple-choice is easier, but writing is a really important skill. In addition, writing assignments teach you to think logically while multiple-choice tests usually mean

   a) regurgitate and forget.

   b) memorize rather than understand.

   c) all of the above.

4. **You'll get more feedback on your writing.** Don't you hate it when you do all that work and the teacher simply writes "B. Good job."? Of course, that's better than "D. What happened?"

3. **Professors are more accessible,** which means it's easier to find a mentor, have opportunities to work on a professor's research, and get meaningful letters of recommendation. At a large college, you'll have to stalk professors and impress them with your knowledge or, at least, your eagerness to learn.

2. **It's easier to get to play on varsity sports teams, host an on-campus radio show, and so on.**

1. **A higher percentage of students graduate within four years,** on average, compared with large colleges.

Top Eight Reasons to Prefer Large Colleges (over 5,000 undergrads)

8. **A large number of specialized courses and majors.** For example, almost all colleges offer a biology major, but a large college might also offer genetics, biophysics, and molecular biology. And within your major, you'll have more choices.

7. Large colleges offer **more teachers to choose from.** But you'll have to make an effort to find out who's good. (See pp. 129–130.)

6. There's **an endless number of students to meet,** often from diverse backgrounds.

5. There are **hundreds of clubs and activities.**

4. On average, **professors are doing more important** research than at small colleges. Graduate students usually get first crack at being research assistants, but if you're a good student and get to know a professor, you may get a chance.

3. You can be a social butterfly or a hermit. At a small college, you usually develop a hard-to-change reputation in the first month. "Oh, Sally. She cheats."

2. Most weekends, you'll have an ample **choice of concerts, movies, lectures, and sports events,** which means you're unlikely to get bored.

1. You may enjoy feeling like part of something big and well known. It somehow feels better to be able to say, "Hi, I go to U.C.L.A." rather than "Hi, I go to Mary Washington College," even though Mary Washington is a fine school.

Living-Learning Program: An option offering some benefits of both large and small colleges

In a living/learning program, a group of 50 to 300 academically motivated students at a large college live in one dorm. Each term, they take one class right in the dorm, usually a small class taught by a top professor who may also live in the dorm. (No, she won't be your roommate.) Also, there are usually special activities. For example, last time I visited Truman State University, on Sunday mornings at its living-learning residence hall, coffee, bagels, and *The New York Times* were available in a central living room in the dorm. Students hung out (some in pajamas) and discussed anything they found interesting in the *Times.* Students in living-learning programs develop especially close bonds with each other because they, a small group, are living, learning, and often sharing meals together. Yet they participate fully in the main university— taking classes there and getting involved in extracurriculars. In short, living/learning programs offer some of the best of big and small schools, often at a public college price.

Some colleges with well-regarded living-learning programs: Michigan State University, University of Maryland (College Park), Indiana University, University of Colorado at Boulder, the University of Illinois at Urbana-Champaign, San Diego State University, University of Wisconsin (Madison), and the University of Michigan at Ann Arbor. Alas, most colleges don't have them.

Now, in light of what you've read, what's best for you? Circle "Small," "Large," or "Living/Learning Program" on your *What I Want* list on p. 7. Before deciding, you might discuss it with your parent or counselor.

DECISION 5: Do I want a college in the sticks or near a large city?

Many students are happier at a college near big-city attractions, such as pro sports, J. Lo in concert, internships at 15 corporations and 26 government agencies, seven Thai restaurants. Also, you don't have to drive three hours to get to a putt-putt airplane that takes you to a connecting flight that takes you to your flight back home.

But some students are happier at a rural college. You can breathe the air, walk without a body alarm, hike nearby, and enjoy a more relaxed pace of life. Most students find that they can survive without a shopping mall, pro sports teams, and multiplexes. And because there's less to do off campus, rural campuses offer a stronger sense of community. But beware: A frequent complaint at rural colleges is "There's nothing to do but drink." After a year or two at rural colleges, some students crave something new. Sometimes, a semester in a domestic or overseas exchange program can restore your sanity.

Now, in light of what you've read, what's best for you? Circle "In/near big city," or "Away from big city" on your *What I Want* list on p. 7. Before deciding, you might discuss it with your parent or counselor.

DECISION 6: Do I want a college near home?

Eighty-five percent of students attend college within a day's drive from home. One reason is the lower transportation costs. But the main reason is that going to college feels less scary to both parent and student if they know that coming home for the weekend is an option.

Why go far away? Because it's fun to experience something different. A California surfer will find New York City an eye-opener—not just the winters, the people. Another plus for faraway colleges is that while a great-fit college might not exist within laundry distance, you're almost sure to find one further away. And it's a little easier to get admitted far away because colleges like a geographically diverse student body.

Now, in light of what you've read, what's best for you? Circle "Northeast," "South," "Midwest," or "West" on your *What I Want* list on p. 8. Before deciding, you might discuss it with your parent or counselor.

DECISION 7: Do I want a college offering many majors or a college that specializes?

Some colleges specialize. For example, Babson College focuses on business. Rose-Hulman specializes in engineering, and Julliard's thing is the performing arts. Don't tell your parents, but in Montreal, there's even a circus college (The National Circus School). Specialty colleges are good choices if you're sure you know what you want to major in. Think about it; if you need a nose job, you're better off with a plastic surgeon than with your general all-purpose scalpel wielder.

Most colleges, however, offer a wide range of majors. These all-purpose institutions are ideal if you're not sure what you want to major in. They may also offer strong programs in specific fields. They're also good if you have a specific major in mind but want to attend a large college. Why? Because most specialty colleges are small.

Now, in light of what you've read, what's best for you? Circle "offer many majors" or "that specialize" on your *What I Want* list on p. 8. Before deciding, you might discuss it with your parent or counselor.

DECISION 8: Do I want a liberal, conservative, or moderate college?

At liberal colleges, the most popular shoes are Birkenstocks or hemp hiking boots. The most popular socks are no socks. The differences are more than superficial. At liberal colleges, most students support reverse discrimination, dislike corporate America, and think it's shallow to lust after a nice car. Fraternities and sororities don't exist or are widely dismissed as dens of elitism, racism, classism, sexism, and homophobia. Courses and extracurriculars are slanted toward save-the-environment themes, the contributions of minorities, and how America should redistribute additional wealth to the poor. There are many student activists and on-campus demonstrations.

At conservative colleges, few students act weird. Most think America is pretty good, and focus more on how to succeed within the system rather than on how to radically change it. At conservative colleges, most students oppose reverse discrimination. Fraternities, sororities, and traditional religion have many adherents, and attitudes toward sex (especially homosexuality) and drugs are conservative, although behavior may not be so conservative.

An Editorial: Why I generally recommend moderate institutions over liberal or conservative ones.

College is supposed to expose you to a wide range of perspectives. Unfortunately, you get a narrow range at many non-moderate (liberal or conservative) institutions. Most lectures and reading assignments are slanted in one direction and students who disagree are made to feel uncomfortable, and perhaps risk a lower grade, so they usually sit silent. Professors who might not teach the party line get fired or aren't hired to begin with. Especially at liberal institutions, this is called *political correctness.*

Now, in light of what you've read, what's best for you? Circle "conservative," "moderate/diverse," or "liberal" on your *What I Want* list on p. 8. Before deciding, you might discuss it with your parent or counselor.

DECISION 9: Do I want to consider single-gender or single-race colleges?

On the plus side, students generally like them. Students form close bonds with each other, and feel a sense of empowerment around race and gender issues. People of their race or gender get to hold all the leadership positions. Although it may be because these colleges attract above-average students, graduates of these colleges do well in the job and graduate school market.

On the downside, you mainly get only your race's or gender's perspective in class discussions. Also, some graduates of single-gender or single-race colleges find it difficult to interact successfully with people not of their race or gender. One reason may simply be that their college provided them with less practice; single-sex or single-race colleges don't mirror the real world. Another reason is that these colleges can cause graduates to have a suspicious or angry attitude toward people not of their race or gender. This, of course, can make life more difficult professionally and personally.

Now, in light of what you've read, what's best for you? If you're interested in single-gender or single-race colleges, circle it on your *What I Want* list on p. 8. Before deciding, you might discuss it with your parent or counselor.

DECISION 10: Do I want to consider strongly religious colleges?

The undergraduate experience at many church-related colleges is not strongly religious. But at strongly religious colleges, your experience will be different. Most students will be of your faith. That can create close bonds and, if you're interested, help you find a mate of similar background. You'll be taking at least a few religion classes, and may be required to attend church. There may be less alcohol use, and probably will be less drug use. There are usually enforced rules that prohibit spending the night in a dorm room of a member of the opposite sex.

The disadvantages of single-gender and single-race colleges cited above may also apply to strongly religious colleges.

Now, in light of what you've read, what's best for you? If you're interested in a strongly religious college, circle it on your *What I Want* list on p. 8. Before deciding, you might discuss it with your parent or counselor.

DECISION 11: Do I care about the college's calendar?

Different colleges have different calendars. Does this matter to you? Read this chart:

CALENDAR	LENGTH OF EACH COURSE	# OF COURSES TAKEN BY GRADUATION
Quarter	10 weeks	60
Semester	15 weeks	40

I prefer the quarter system because you get to try out more courses and they're shorter. If you really like a course or a professor, you usually can take another, but if you can't stand the course, you're only stuck for ten weeks. The main reason to prefer a college that has a semester calendar is if you're concerned that midterms, finals, and term papers will come too quickly in a ten-week quarter.

The 4-1-4 calendar is sort of a compromise. The courses are halfway between semesters and quarters in length. (This gets confusing now.) Each year, you take 5 courses for 4 months, 1 course during a 1-month interterm, then 5 courses for 4 months. That's why it's called 4-1-4. Most students like the one-month interterm because you can focus, undistracted, on one hard or interesting course, and because fun courses are offered, for example, a "study" trip to Mexico. Or you can take an independent study. One student got interterm course credit for visiting six football stadiums and writing a paper about their differences.

The ultimate opportunity to focus is the block calendar. You take a total of 40 courses, just like at a semester-calendar college. The difference is that you take just one course at a time. Most students either love it or hate it. You'll love it if you'd enjoy immersing yourself in one subject for three and a half weeks, then moving to something else for three and a half weeks, and so on. It can be a nightmare for procrastinators and no picnic for science majors—try learning a semester's worth of organic chemistry in three and a half weeks.

The block calendar is offered only by a few colleges, notably Colorado College (that's not the University of Colorado) and Cornell College (the one in Iowa, not New York).

Now, in light of what you've read, what's best for you? Circle "quarter," "semester," "4-1-4," or "block" on your *What I Want* list on p. 9. Before deciding, you might discuss it with your parent or counselor.

DECISION 12: Do I want a college that offers a co-op program?

In a co-op program, you get course credit for doing a paid internship for a company or the government, under a professor's supervision.

Co-op is good because you get to apply classroom theory in a real-world setting. It helps you figure out what you want to be when you grow up. Your pay can help you to graduate from college with less loan to pay back, and co-op often leads to a good job after graduation. But because co-op yields little course credit for the many hours involved, co-op students often need an extra year to graduate.

Now, in light of what you've read, what's best for you? If you want to consider colleges with co-op programs, circle it on your *What I Want* list on p. 9. Before deciding, you might discuss it with your parent or a counselor.

DECISION 13: Do I need a college with extensive disability services?

The Americans with Disabilities Act requires all colleges receiving federal funds (nearly all colleges do) to provide services for the disabled. But some colleges offer much more than the minimum. Take, for example, services for the learning disabled. While most colleges provide tutoring, other colleges add note-takers, voice-input word processors, computers that scan printed material and then read it aloud, course books on tape, special advisors, and summer programs. Students with learning disabilities might want to consult the *K & W Guide to Colleges for the Learning Disabled*.

Now, in light of what you've read, what's best for you? If you want a college with extensive disability services, circle that item on your *What I Want* list on p. 9. Before deciding, you might want to discuss it with your parent or a counselor.

Appendix B

The Colleges

Listed here are 434 colleges—noteworthy enough that they attract a significant percentage of students from beyond a 200-mile radius. Many other colleges, especially those close to home, can also be wise choices. If you don't know about your close-to-home colleges, see your counselor.

IMPORTANT! In all cases, Web addresses begin with *www.* All data was current as this book went to press. Check with the college's web site for any changes.

CODES

$	Total four-year cost of under $75,000
$$	Total four-year cost of $75,000–$105,000
$$$	Total four-year cost of $105,000–$135,000
$$$$	Total four-year cost of $135,000–$160,000
$$$$$	Total four-year cost of more than $160,000

a	African American/black	r	strongly religious
c	conservative	m	men's
d	special learning disability program	o	block calendar
		q	quarter calendar
f	4-1-4- calendar (or similar calendar)	T	Tribal
		t	trimester calendar
l	liberal	v	cooperative education
L	living/learning program	w	women's

Cost is defined as the 2003–2004 published tuition, fees, average room and board, plus an estimate of the average amount students spend on books and living expenses: recreation, clothes, travel to and from home, and so on. A 3 percent annual increase for years two through four is also included. Where two figures are provided, the first is for in-state residents. Remember that some families can get significant financial aid. (See Chapter 5.)

A "small" college is defined as under 5,000 full-time equivalent undergraduates.

The decision to describe a college as "liberal," "conservative," or "strongly religious" was made by synthesizing the input of counselors, college guides, and the author. Colleges marked as liberal or conservative are unquestionably so. Many other colleges, including most of the nation's hardest-to-get-into, are generally liberal.

TWO-YEAR COLLEGES

Unless otherwise noted, all are small, away from big cities, and have students who mainly got Bs and Cs in high school.

NORTHEAST

Don't forget about your local colleges. (Need ideas? See your counselor.)

Becker $$$ (suburban) v MA beckercollege.edu 877-523-2537

Dean $$$ MA dean.edu 508-541-1900

Harcum $$ w PA harcum.edu 610-525-4100

Keystone $$$ d PA keystone.edu 877-426-5534

Newbury $$$ v (suburban) MA newbury.edu 800-NEWBURY

Paul Smith's $$ NY paulsmiths.edu 800-421-2605

Sage Junior of Albany $$$ (urban) NY sage.edu/sca 888-837-9724

Hartford College for Women $$$ (suburban) CT 800-947-4303

Landmark $$$$$ (town) d VT landmark.edu 802-387-4767

Mitchell $$$ d (incl. L.D program fee) CT mitchell.edu, 800-443-2811

SOUTH

Don't forget about your local colleges. (Need ideas? See your counselor.)

Brevard $$ (town) d NC brevard.edu, 800-527-9090 (also offers 4-year programs)

MIDWEST

Don't forget about your local colleges. (Need ideas? See your counselor.)

Sisseton-Wahpeton $ qT (no room and board) SD swcc.cc.sd.us 605-698-3966

Vincennes U. $/$ d IN vinu.edu 800-742-9198

Cottey $$ w MO cottey.edu 888-5-COTTEY

Lincoln $$ IL lincolncollege.edu 217-732-3155

Waldorf $$ v IA waldorf.edu 800-292-1903

WEST

Don't forget about your local colleges. (Need ideas? See your counselor.)

Dixie $/$ UT dixie.edu 888-GO-2-DIXIE

Yavapai $/$ AZ yavapai.cc.az.us 800-922-6787

Marymount $$$ (suburban), CA marymountpv.edu 310-377-5501

Mount St. Mary's $$$ (urban) CA msmc.la.edu 310-954-4000

Four-Year Colleges That Offer Many Majors

Unless otherwise noted, all have a politically/socially moderate or diverse student body, are not strongly religious, have men and women students, run on a semester calendar, and do not offer co-op programs.

Mainly A students, small, Northeast, in or near a big city

Bryn Mawr $$$$$ w PA brynmawr.edu 800-BMC-1885

Columbia $$$$$ l NY college.columbia.edu 212-854-1754

Haverford $$$$$ PA haverford.edu 610-896-1000

Johns Hopkins $$$$$ fv MD jhu.edu 410-516-8000

Swarthmore $$$$$ l PA swarthmore.edu 800-667-3110

Wellesley $$$$$ w MA wellesley.edu 781-283-1000

Mainly A students, small, Northeast, town

Amherst $$$$$ t MA amherst.edu 413-542-2000

Bates College $$$$$ f ME bates.edu 207-786-6255

Bowdoin $$$$$ ME bowdoin.edu 207-725-3000

Middlebury $$$$$ f VT middlebury.edu 802-443-5000

Wesleyan U. $$$$$ lv CT wesleyan.edu 860-685-2000

Williams $$$$$ f MA williams.edu 413-597-3131

Mainly A students, small, South, in or near a big city

Rice $$$$ TX rice.edu 800-527-OWLS

Mainly A students, small, South, town
Washington & Lee U. $$$$ cf VA wlu.edu 540-458-8400

Mainly A students, small, Midwest, in or near a big city
U. of Chicago $$$$$ Lq IL uchicago.edu 773-702-1234

Mainly A students, small, Midwest, town
Carleton $$$$ lt MN carleton.edu 800-995-2275

Oberlin $$$$$ lf OH oberlin.edu 800-622-OBIE

Mainly A students, small, West, in or near a big city
Claremont McKenna $$$$$ t CA claremontmckenna.edu
   909-621-8088

Pomona $$$$$ CA pomona.edu 909-621-8000

Reed $$$$$ l OR reed.edu 800-547-4750

Mainly A students, small, West, town
Deep Springs (a two-year college) $ lm 6 7-week terms
   CA deepsprings.edu 760-872-2000

Mainly A students, large, Northeast, in or near a big city
Brown U. $$$$$ dlq RI brown.edu 401-863-1000

Georgetown $$$$$ d DC georgetown.edu 202-687-0100

Harvard $$$$$ L MA fas.harvard.edu 617-495-1000

Massachusetts Institute of Technology $$$$$ fv MA web.mit.edu
   617-253-1000

Princeton $$$$$ NJ princeton.edu 609-258-3000

Tufts $$$$$ MA tufts.edu 617-628-5000

U. of Pennsylvania $$$$$ f PA upenn.edu 215-898-5000

Yale U. $$$$$ L CT yale.edu 203-432-4771

Mainly A students, large, Northeast, town
Cornell U. $$$/$$$$$ (public part) $$$$$ (private part) dv NY
   cornell.edu 607-255-5241

Dartmouth $$$$$ q NH dartmouth.edu 603-646-1110

Mainly A students, large, South, in or near a big city
Duke $$$$$ NC duke.edu 919-684-8111

Mainly A students, large, South, town
College of William and Mary $/$$$$ v VA wm.edu 757-221-4000

Mainly A students, large, Midwest, in or near a big city
Northwestern $$$$$ qv IL northwestern.edu 847-491-3741

Mainly A students, large, Midwest, town
U. of Notre Dame $$$$$ d IN nd.edu 219-631-5000

Mainly A students, large, West, in or near a big city
U. of California, Berkeley $$/$$$$ dlv CA berkeley.edu
    510-642-6000
U. of California, Los Angeles $$/$$$$ dq CA ucla.edu
    310-825-4321
Stanford $$$$$ dq CA stanford.edu 650-723-2300

Mainly A students, large, West, town
None

Mainly B to A students, small, Northeast, in or near a big city
Barnard $$$$$ lwt NY barnard.edu 212-854-5262
Brandeis $$$$$ lq MA brandeis.edu 800-622-0622
College of the Holy Cross $$$$$ r MA holycross.edu
    800-442-2421
Sarah Lawrence $$$$$ l NY sarahlawrence.edu 800-888-2858
Trinity $$$$$ CT trincoll.edu 860-297-2000
Union $$$$$ t NY union.edu 888-843-6688

Mainly B to A students, small, Northeast, town
Grove City $$ c PA gcc.edu 724-458-2000
St. Mary's College of Maryland $/$$ MD smcm.edu 800-492-7181
Bard College $$$$$ lf NY bard.edu 845-758-6822

Bucknell University $$$$$ c PA bucknell.edu 570-577-2000

Colby $$$$$ f ME colby.edu 800-723-3032

Colgate $$$$$ NY colgate.edu 315-228-1000

Connecticut College $$$$$ CT conncoll.edu 860-439-2000

Franklin and Marshall $$$$$ PA fandm.edu 717-291-3951

Gettysburg $$$$$ PA gettysburg.edu 800-431-0803

Hamilton $$$$$ NY hamilton.edu 800-843-2655

Lafayette $$$$$ f PA lafayette.edu 610-330-5100

Mount Holyoke $$$$$ wf PA mtholyoke.edu 413-538-2000

St. John's $$$$$ MD sjca.edu 800-727-9238

Simon's Rock College of Bard $$$$$ MA simons-rock.edu
    413-528-0771

Smith $$$$$ w MA smith.edu 413-584-2700

Vassar $$$$$ NY vassar.edu 800-827-7270

Mainly B to A students, small, South, in or near a big city
New College of the U. of South Florida $/$$$ lf FL ncf.edu
    941-359-4269

Trinity U. $$$ TX trinity.edu 800-TRINITY

Rhodes $$$$ TN rhodes.edu 800-844-5969

U. of Richmond $$$$ c VA richmond.edu 800-700-1662

Wake Forest U. $$$$ NC wfu.edu 336-758-5000

Mainly B to A students, small, South, town
Mary Washington $/$$ v VA mwc.edu 800-468-5614

U. of the South $$$$ c TN sewanee.edu 800-522-2234

Davidson $$$$ NC cr davidson.edu 800-768-0380

Mainly B to A students, small, Midwest, in or
near a big city
Case Western Reserve $$$$ qv OH cwru.edu 216-368-2000

Colorado College $$$$$ lo CO coloradocollege.edu 800-542-7214

Macalester $$$$ lf MN macalester.edu 800-231-7974

Mainly B to A students, small, Midwest, town
U. of Minnesota, Morris q **$$/$$** MN mrs.umn.edu 800-992-8863

Grinnell **$$$$** l IA grinnell.edu 800-247-0113

Kenyon **$$$$** OH kenyon.edu 800-848-2468

Mainly B to A students, small, West, in or near a big city
Occidental **$$$$$** l CA oxy.edu 800-825-5262

Mainly B to A students, small, West, town
none

Mainly B to A students, large, Northeast, in or near a big city
McGill University **$** (Canadians)/**$** Non-Canadians) CANADA
mcgill.ca 514-398-4455

U. of Toronto **$** (Canadians) **$** (Non-Canadians) CANADA utoronto.ca
416-978-2011

College of New Jersey **$$/$$$** NJ tcnj.edu 800-624-0967

Rutgers **$$/$$$** NJ rutgers.edu 732-932-4636

Boston College **$$$$$** MA bc.edu 800-360-2522

Carnegie Mellon **$$$$$** v PA cmu.edu 412-268-2000

New York U. **$$$$$** NY nyu.edu 212-998-1212

U. of Rochester **$$$$$** rochester.edu NY 888-822-2256

State U. of New York at Buffalo: **$$/$$** buffalo.edu 888-UB-ADMIT

Mainly B to A students, large, Northeast, town
Queen's University **$$** (Canadians) **$$$** (Non-Canadians) CANADA
queensu.ca 613-533-2000

State U. of New York at Binghamton **$/$$** NY binghamton.edu
607-777-2000

State U. of New York, College at Geneseo **$$/$$** NY geneseo.edu
585-245-5211

Pennsylvania State U., Main Campus v **$$/$$$** PA psu.edu
814-865-5471

U. of Vermont $$/$$$$ vd VT uvm.edu 802-656-3131

Lehigh $$$$$ v PA lehigh.edu 610-758-3100

Mainly B to A students, large, South, in or near a big city

U. of Texas at Austin $/$$ TX utexas.edu 512-471-3434

U. of North Carolina, Chapel Hill $/$$$ NC unc.edu
919-962-2211

Emory $$$$$ GA emory.edu 800-727-6036

Tulane $$$$$ LA tulane.edu 800-873-9283

Vanderbilt U. $$$$$ TN vanderbilt.edu 800-288-0432

Mainly B to A students, large, South, town

U. of Virginia $/$$$$ d VA virginia.edu 434-924-0311

Mainly B to A students, large, Midwest, in or near a big city

U. of Wisconsin, Madison $/$$ v WI wisc.edu 608-262-1234

University of Michigan $$/$$$$ dtv MI umich.edu 734-764-1817

Washington U. $$$$$ v MO wustl.edu 800-638-0700

Mainly B to A students, large, Midwest, town

Truman State $/$$ MO truman.edu 800-892-7792

Miami U. $$/$$$ v OH muohio.edu 513-529-1809

Mainly B to A students, large, West, in or near a big city

U. of California, San Diego $$/$$$$ q CA ucsd.edu 858-534-8273

Mainly B to A students, large, West, town

California Polytechnic State U, San Luis Obispo $/$$$ dqv CA
calpoly.edu 805-756-1111

U. of California, Davis $$/$$$$ dq CA ucdavis.edu 530-752-1011

Many B– students, small, Northeast, in or near a big city

Don't forget about your local colleges. (Need ideas? See your counselor.)

Trent $ (Canadians) $ (Non-Canadians) l CANADA trentu.ca
705-748-1011

American International $$$ d MA aic.edu 800-242-3142

Mercyhurst $$$ tvd PA mercyhurst.edu 814-824-2000

Catholic U. of America $$$$$ r DC cua.edu 800-673-2772

Clark $$$$ l MA clarku.edu 800-462-5275

Curry $$$$ qd MA curry.edu 617-333-2210

Iona $$$$ fd NY iona.edu 800-231-IONA

Loyola $$$$$ MD loyola.edu 800-221-9107

Muhlenberg $$$$ PA muhlenberg.edu 484-664-3100

New England College $$$$ qd NH nec.edu 800-521-7642

Wagner $$$$ NY wagner.edu 718-390-3100

Drew $$$$$ NJ drew.edu 973-408-3000

Eugene Lang $$$$$ I NY lang.edu 877-528-3321

Goucher $$$$ MD goucher.edu 800-GOUCHER

Simmons $$$$$ w MA simmons.edu 800-345-8468

Skidmore $$$$$ NY skidmore.edu 800-867-6007

Many B– students, small, Northeast, town

Don't forget about your local colleges. (Need ideas? See your counselor.)

Acadia $$ (Canadians)/$$ (Non-Canadians) CANADA acadiau.ca 902-542-2201

Mount Allison $ (Canadians)/$$ Non-Canadians) CANADA mta.ca 506-364-2269

Ramapo $$/$$$ v NJ ramapo.edu 800-972-6276

Pennsylvania State U. at Erie, Behrend College $$/$$$ PA pserie.psu.edu 866-374-3378

College of the Atlantic $$$ lqv ME coa.edu 800-528-0025

Siena $$$ crq NY siena.edu 518-783-2300

Southern Vermont $ d VT svc.edu 800-378-2782

Elizabethtown $$$$ PA etown.edu 717-361-1400

Goddard $$ lv VT goddard.edu 800-468-4888

Gordon-$$$ cr MA gordon.edu 800-343-1379

Quinnipiac $$$$ CT quinnipiac.edu 800-462-1944

St. Anselm's $$$$ NH anselm.edu 888-4ANSELM

St. Joseph's $$$$ v PA sju.edu 888-232-4295

St. Michael's $$$$ VT smcvt.edu 800-762-8000

Salve Regina $$$$ RI salve.edu 888-GO-SALVE

Susquehanna $$$$ c PA susqu.edu 570-374-0101

U. of New England $$$ dv ME une.edu 800-477-4UNE

Ursinus $$$$ PA ursinus.edu 610-409-3200

Washington College $$$$$ MD washcoll.edu 800-422-1782

McDaniel $$$$ MD wmdc.edu 800-638-5005

Alfred $$$$ qv NY alfred.edu 800-541-9229

Allegheny $$$$ lq PA allegheny.edu 800-521-5293

Bennington $$$$$ l VT bennington.edu 800-833-6845

Dickinson $$$$$ PA dickinson.edu 800-644-1773

Hampshire $$$$$ lf MA hampshire.edu 877-937-4267

Hartwick $$$$ t NY hartwick.edu 888-427-8942

Hobart and William Smith $$$$$ t NY hws.edu 800-245-0100

Manhattanville $$$$ NY 800-328-4553 manhattanville.edu

Marlboro $$$$ VT t marlboro.edu 802-343-0049

St. Lawrence $$$$$ NY stlawu.edu 800-285-1856

Wheaton $$$$$ MA wheatoncollege.edu 800-394-6003

Many B– students, small, South, in or near a big city

Don't forget about your local colleges. (Need ideas? See your counselor.)

The Citadel $/$$ c SC citadel.edu 800-868-1842

Hendrix $$$ t AR hendrix.edu 800-277-9017

Xavier U. of Louisiana $$ av LA xula.edu 877-928-4378

Birmingham-Southern College cf $$$ AL bsc.edu 800-523-5793

Millsaps $$$ MS millsaps.edu 800-352-1050

Morehouse $$$ amv GA morehouse.edu 800-851-1254

Our Lady of the Lake v $$$ TX ollusa.edu 800-436-6558

Samford $$ crfv AL samford.edu 800-888-7218

Spelman $$$ wa GA spelman.edu 800-982-2411

St. Edward's $$$ v TX stedwards.edu 800-555-0164

Thomas More $$$ cv KY thomasmore.edu 800-825-4557

Transylvania $$$ f KY transy.edu 800-872-6798

U. of Dallas $$$ cr TX udallas.edu 800-628-6999

Wofford $$$ cfv SC wofford.edu 864-597-4130

Agnes Scott $$$$ wt GA agnesscott.edu 800-868-8602

Eckerd $$$$ f FL eckerd.edu 800-456-9009

Furman $$$$ crtv SC furman.edu 864-294-2034

Guilford $$$ NC guilford.edu 800-992-7759

Hollins $$$$ wf VA hollins.edu 800-456-9595

Oglethorpe $$$$ v GA oglethorpe.edu 800-428-4484

Rollins $$$$$ f FL rollins.edu 407-646-2161

Many B– students, small, South, town
Don't forget about your local colleges. (Need ideas? See your counselor.)

College of the Ozarks $ df MO cofo.edu 800-222-0525

Berea $ f KY berea.edu 800-326-5948

U. of Montevallo $/$ AL montevallo.edu 800-292-4349

U. of North Carolina, Asheville $/$$ NC unca.edu 800-531-9842

Winthrop $/$$ v SC winthrop.edu 800-763-0230

Flagler $ FL flagler.edu 800-304-4208 x220

Lenoir-Rhyne $$$ c NC lrc.edu 800-277-5721

Austin $$$ f TX austincollege.edu 800-442-5363

Catawba $$$ NC catawba.edu 800-228-2922

Centre $$$ f KY centre.edu 800-423-6236

Davis and Elkins $$ dv WV davisandelkins.edu 800-624-3157

Elon $$$ fv NC elon.edu 800-334-8448

Emory and Henry $$$ VA ehc.edu 800-848-5493

Presbyterian $$$ SC presby.edu 864-833-8230

Southwestern $$$ TX southwestern.edu 800-252-3166

St. Andrew's Presbyterian $$ f NC sapc.edu 910-277-5555

Warren Wilson $$$ l NC warren-wilson.edu 800-934-3536

Hampden-Sydney cm $$$$ VA hsc.edu 800-755-0733

Lynn $$$$ d FL lynn.edu 800-888-5966

Randolph-Macon Woman's College w $$$$ VA rmwc.edu
   800-745-7692

Sweet Briar $$$ cwf VA sbc.edu 800-381-6142

West Virginia Wesleyan df $$$ WV wvwc.edu 800-722-9933

Many B– students, small, Midwest, in or near a big city
Don't forget about your local colleges. (Need ideas? See your counselor.)

Alverno $$ wv WI alverno.edu 800-933-3401

Calvin $$$ crfv MI calvin.edu 800-668-0122

Concordia $$$ q MI cuaa.edu 800-253-0680

Nebraska Wesleyan $$$ cq NE nebrwesleyan.edu
   800-541-3818

Ohio Dominican $$$ OH ohiodominican.edu 800-854-2670

Oral Roberts $$ cr OK oru.edu 00-678-8876

St. Norbert $$$ v WI snc.edu 800-236-4878

Stephens $$$ w MO stephens.edu 800-876-7207

U. of Tulsa $$$ OK utulsa.edu 800-331-3050

Wheaton $$$ cr IL wheaton.edu 800-222-2419

William Jewell $$$ c MO jewell.edu 800-753-7009

Kalamazoo $$$$ qv MI kzoo.edu 800-253-3602

Lake Forest $$$$ IL lakeforest.edu 800-828-4751

U. of Denver $$$$ dqv CO du.edu 800-525-9495

Wittenberg U. $$$$ t OH wittenberg.edu 800-677-7558

Many B– students, small, Midwest, town
Don't forget about your local colleges. (Need ideas? See your counselor.)

Oglala Lakota $ T (no room and board) SD olc.edu
   605-455-6000

Sinte Gleska $ T (no room and board) SD sinte.edu 605-747-2263

Shimer $$ (no board) v IL shimer.edu 800-215-7173

Adrian $$$ v MI adrian.edu 800-877-2246

Alma $$$ f MI alma.edu 800-321-ALMA

Baker U $$$ f KS bakeru.edu 800-873-4282

Barat $$$ d IL barat.edu 847-234-3000

Buena Vista, $$$ f IA bvu.edu 712-749-2235

Carroll $$$ v MT carroll.edu 800-99-ADMIT

Carroll $$$ WI cc.edu 800-CARROLL

Hanover $$$ f IN hanover.edu 800-213-2178

Hillsdale $$$ cq MI hillsdale.edu 517-607-2327

Loras $$$ d IA loras.edu 800-24-LORAS

Muskingum $$$ d OH muskingum.edu 800-752-6082

Rocky Mountain v $$ MT rocky.edu 800-877-6259

St. John's/St. Benedict mwf $$$ MN csbsju.edu 800-544-1489

U. of Evansville $$$ cv IN evansville.edu 800-423-8633

Valparaiso U. crv $$$ IN valpo.edu 888-468-2576

Wartburg $$$ f IA wartburg.edu 800-772-2085

Westminster College d $$ MO westminster-mo.edu 800-475-3361

Albion $$$ MI albion.edu 517-629-1000

Antioch $$$$ lqv OH antioch-college.edu 800-543-9436

Beloit $$$$ WI beloit.edu 800-923-5648

Butler $$$$ IN butler.edu 888-940-8100

College of Wooster $$$$ OH wooster.edu 800-877-9905

Cornell $$$ o IA cornellcollege.edu 800-747-1112

Denison $$$$$ f OH denison.edu 800-DENISON

DePauw $$$$ f IN depauw.edu 800-447-2495

Earlham $$$$ lq IN earlham.edu 800-327-5426

Gustavus Adolphus fv $$$ MN gustavus.edu 800-GUSTAVUS

Hiram $$$$ q OH hiram.edu 800-362-5280

Illinois Wesleyan f $$$$ IL iwu.edu 800-332-2498

Knox $$$$ t IL knox.edu 800-678-KNOX

Lawrence $$$$ t WI lawrence.edu 800-227-0982

Ohio Wesleyan $$$$ OH owu.edu 800-922-8953

Ripon $$$ WI ripon.edu 800-947-4766

St. Olaf $$$$ f MN 800-800-3025

Wabash $$$$ cm IN wabash.edu 800-345-5385

Many B– students, small, West, in or near a big city
Don't forget about your local colleges. (Need ideas? See your counselor.)

Gonzaga $$$ WA 800-986-2584

Lewis and Clark $$$$ lq OR lclark.edu 800-444-4111

Loyola Marymount $$$$ CA lmu.edu 310-338-2750

Mills $$$$ lvw CA mills.edu 800-87-MILLS

Pacific Lutheran $$$ fv WA plu.edu 800-274-6758

Santa Clara $$$$$ qv CA scu.edu 408-554-4700

St. Mary's College of California f $$$$ CA stmarys-ca.edu
   800-800-4SMC

U. of Portland $$$$ v OR up.edu 888-627-5601

U. of Puget Sound v $$$$ WA ups.edu 800-396-7191

U. of San Diego $$/$$$$ r CA ucsd.edu 858-534-4831

Pepperdine $$$$$ cr CA pepperdine.edu 310-506-4392

Pitzer $$$$$ CA pitzer.edu lv 800-748-9371

Scripps $$$$$ w CA scrippscollege.edu 800-770-1333

St. John's $$$$$ NM sjcsf.edu 800-331-5232

Willamette U. $$$$ OR willamette.edu 877-542-2787

Many B– students, small, West, town
Don't forget about your local colleges. (Need ideas? See your counselor.)

Fort Lewis $/$$ tv CO fortlewis.edu 970-247-7184

Grand Canyon $$$ r AZ grand-canyon.edu 602-589-2855

Albertson $$ ID albertson.edu 800-AC-IDAHO.

College of Santa Fe $$$ NM csf.edu 800-456-2673

Hawaii Pacific fv $$$ HI hpu.edu 800-669-4724

Linfield $$$$ f OR linfield.edu 800-640-2287

Thomas Aquinas $$$ c CA thomasaquinas.edu 800-634-9797

Westmont $$$$$ cr CA westmont.edu 805-565-6000

Whitman $$$$ WA whitman.edu 877-462-9448

Whitworth $$$$ cfrv WA whitworth.edu 509-777-3212

U. of Redlands $$$$ fv CA redlands.edu 800-455-5064

Many B– students, large, Northeast, in or near a big city

Don't forget about your local colleges. (Need ideas? See your counselor.)

State U. of New York, Albany $$/$$ NY albany.edu 800-293-7869

U. of Maryland, College Park $$/$$$ v MD maryland.edu
  800-422-5867

Adelphi $$$ d NY adelphi.edu 800-ADELPHI

Hofstra $$$$ df NY hofstra.edu 800-HOFSTRA

Howard U. $$ a DC howard.edu 800-822-6363

Duquesne $$$$ v PA duq.edu 800-456-0590

Fordham $$$$$ NY fordham.edu 800-FORDHAM

Long Island U. Post campus $$$$$ dv NY: liu.edu 516-299-2900

American U. $$$$$ dv DC american.edu 202-885-6000

Boston U. $$$$$ dv MA bu.edu 617-353-2300

Syracuse $$$$$ v NY syracuse.edu 315-443-3611

Villanova U. $$$$$ PA villanova.edu 610-519-4000

Many B– students, large, Northeast, town

Don't forget about your local colleges. (Need ideas? See your counselor.)

Indiana U. of Pennsylvania $/$$ v PA iup.edu 800-442-6830

Millersville U. of Pennsylvania $/$$ fv PA millersville.edu
  800-MU-ADMIT

Shippensburg U. of Pennsylvania $/$$ PA ship.edu 800-822-8028

U. of Maine, Orono $/$$ v ME umaine.edu 877-486-2364

State U. of New York at Stony Brook $/$$ NY stonybrook.edu
  800-872-7869

U. of Connecticut $$/$$$ v CT uconn.edu 860-486-3137

U. of Delaware $$/$$$ fv DE udel.edu 302-831-8123

U. of Massachusetts, Amherst MA $$/$$$ MA umass.edu
  413-545-0222

U. of New Hampshire $$/$$$ NH unh.edu 603-862-1360

Ithaca $$$$ NY ithaca.edu 800-429-4274

Many B– students, large, South, in or near a big city

Don't forget about your local colleges. (Need ideas? See your counselor.)

College of Charleston $$/$$$ v SC cofc.edu 843-953-5670

Florida State U. $/$$ v FL fsu.edu 850-644-6200

Louisiana State $/$$ v LA lsu.edu 225-578-1175

U. of Kentucky $/$$ v KY uky.edu 859-257-2000

U. of South Carolina, Columbia $/$$$ v SC sc.edu 800-868-5USC

U. of Tennessee, Knoxville $/$$ v KY tennessee.edu 800-221-8657

U. of Alabama (Tuscaloosa) $/$$ v AL ua.edu 800-933-BAMA

U. of Florida $/$$ dv FL ufl.edu 352-392-1365

Baylor University $$$ cr TX baylor.edu 800-BAYLORU

Texas Christian $$$ c TX tcu.edu 800-TCU-3764

Southern Methodist $$$$ cv TX smu.edu 800-323-0672

U. of Miami $$$$$ FL miami.edu 305-284-4323

Many B– students, large, South, town

Don't forget about your local colleges. (Need ideas? See your counselor.)

Georgia Southern $/$$ cqv GA gasou.edu 912-681-5391

U. of Mississippi $/$ MS olemiss.edu 800-653-6477

Appalachian State U. $/$$ NC appstate.edu 828-262-2120

Auburn U. $/$$ v AL auburn.edu 800-282-8769

Austin Peay $/$$ TN apsu.edu 800-844-2778

Clemson $/$$ v SC clemson.edu 864-656-2287

Texas A & M $/$$ cv TX: tamu.edu 979-845-3741

U. of Arkansas, $/$$ v AR uark.edu 800-377-UOFA

U. of Georgia $/$$$ dqv GA uga.edu 706-542-2112

West Virginia U. $/$$ v WV wvu.edu 800-344-9881

Virginia Polytechnic Institute and State U. $/$$ v VA vt.edu
540-231-6267

James Madison $/$$ VA jmu.edu 540-568-5681

Many B– students, large, Midwest, in or near a big city

Don't forget about your local colleges. (Need ideas? See your counselor.)

Fort Hays State $/$$ d KS fhsu.edu 800-628-3478

U. of Iowa $/$$$ v IA uiowa.edu 800-553-4692

U. of Kansas $/$$ v KS ku.edu 785-864-3911

U. of Missouri, Columbia $/$$$ v MO missouri.edu 800-225-6075

U. of Nebraska, Lincoln $/$$ v NE unl.edu 800-742-8800

U. of Oklahoma $/$$ v OK ou.edu 800-234-6868

Colorado State $/$$ dv CO colostate.edu 970-491-6909

Michigan State $/$$$ v MI msu.edu 517-355-8332

Ohio State $$/$$$ dqv OH csu.edu 614-292-3980

U. of Minnesota, Twin Cities $$/$$$ qv MN umn.edu/tc 800-752-1000

University of Waterloo $ (Canadians)/$$ (Non-Canadians) tv CANADA
uwaterloo.ca 519-888-4567

Western Michigan U. $/$$ v MI wmich.edu 800-400-4WMU

U. of Illinois, Urbana-Champaign $$/$$ v IL uiuc.edu 217-333-0302

U. of Colorado at Boulder $/$$$ dv CO colorado.edu 303-492-6301

Bradley $$$ v IL bradley.edu 800-447-6460

Creighton $$$$ c NE creighton.edu 800-282-5835

De Paul $$$$ dq IL depaul.edu 800-4DEPAUL

U. of Dayton $$$ v OH udayton.edu 800-837-7433

U. of St. Thomas $$$$ f MN stthomas.edu 800-328-6819 x26150

Drake $$$ v IA drake.edu 800-44-DRAKE

Marquette $$$$ WI marquette.edu 800-222-6544

Many B– students, large, Midwest, town

Don't forget about your local colleges. (Need ideas? See your counselor.)

Ohio U. $$/$$$ qv OH ohiou.edu 740-593-4100

Southern Illinois U. $/$$ dv IL siuc.edu 618-453-4381

U. of Wisconsin, Eau Claire $/$$ f WI uwec.edu 715-836-5415

U. of Wyoming $/$$ v WY uwyo.edu 800-DIAL-WYO

Purdue $/$$$ v IN purdue.edu 765-494-1776

Indiana U. $$/$$$ v IN indiana.edu 812-855-0661

Many B– students, large, West, in or near a big city

Don't forget about your local colleges. (Need ideas? See your counselor.)

Brigham Young University $ crfv UT byu.edu 801-422-2507

Arizona State U. $/$$$ dv AZ asu.edu 480-965-7788

U. of Arizona $/$$$ dv AZ arizona.edu 520-621-3237

U. of British Columbia $ (Canadians) $$$ (Non-Canadians) CANADA
ubc.ca 877-272-1422

U. of Nevada, Las Vegas $/$$ dv NV unlv.edu 702-895-2030

U. of New Mexico $/$$ v NM unm.edu 800-225-5866

U. of Utah $/$$ qv UT utah.edu 801-581-7281

U. of Oregon $/$$$ dq OR uoregon.edu 800-232-3825

U. of Washington $$/$$$ qv WA washington.edu 206-543-9686

U. of Hawaii at Manoa $/$$ v HI uhm.hawaii.edu 800-823-9771

U. of California, Santa Barbara $$/$$$$ qv CA ucsb.edu
805-893-2881

U. of Southern California $$$$$ dv CA usc.edu 213-740-1111

Many B– students, large, West, town

Don't forget about your local colleges. (Need ideas? See your counselor.)

Evergreen State $/$$$ lqv WA evergreen.edu 360-867-6170

University of Idaho $/$$ v ID uidaho.edu 888-884-3246

University of Montana $/$$ v MT umt.edu 800-462-8636

Western Washington U. $/$$ qv WA wwu.edu 360-650-3440

California State U., Stanislaus $/$$ fv CA csustan.edu 800-300-7420

Humboldt State University $/$$ lqv CA humboldt.edu 707-826-4402

Oregon State $/$$$ qv OR oregonstate.edu 800-291-4192

Sonoma State $/$$$ d CA sonoma.edu 707-664-2778

U. of California, Santa Cruz $$/$$$$ lq CA ucsc.edu 831-459-4008

Four-Year Colleges That Specialize in Certain Majors

Note: These colleges focus just on a few popular careers. Other career-specific colleges and technical institutes specialize in such careers as nursing, photography, and culinary arts (chef). To find out more about these, check with your counselor or with a local two-year college.

Military Institutions

United States Air Force Academy $0 c CO usafa.edu 800-443-9266

United States Coast Guard Academy $0 c CT cga.edu 800-883-8724

United States Military Academy $0 c NY usma.edu 845-938-4041

United States Merchant Marine Academy $0 c NY usmma.edu 866-546-4778

United States Naval Academy $0 c MD usna.edu 410-293-4361

Institutions specializing in engineering and physical sciences

(Unless otherwise noted, all are four-year, small, suburban/urban, and require a solid B average.)

Don't forget about your local colleges. (Need ideas? See your counselor.)

Montana Tech $/$$ cq MT mtech.edu 800-445-TECH

Georgia Institute of Technology (large, mainly A students) $/$$$ qv GA gatech.edu 404-894-4154

Cooper Union $$ (mainly A students) NY cooper.edu 212-353-4120

California Maritime Academy $/$$$ c CA csum.edu 800-561-1945

Michigan Technological U. $/$$$ qv MI mtu.edu 888-688-1885

U. of Missouri, Rolla $/$$$ v MO umr.edu 800-522-0938

Colorado School of Mines $$/$$$$ v CO mines.edu 800-446-9488

Kettering University $$$ tv MI kettering.edu 800-955-4464

California Institute of Technology (all A students) $$$$$ t CA caltech.edu 800-568-8324

Clarkson $$$$ v NY clarkson.edu 800-248-7448

Rose-Hulman Institute of Technology cq $$$$ IN rose-hulman.edu 800-248-7448

Worcester Polytechnic Institute **$$$$** v 4 7-week terms MA wpi.edu
508-831-5286

Harvey Mudd (mainly A students) **$$$$$** CA hmc.edu 909-621-8011

Massachusetts Institute of Technology (mainly A students, large)
$$$$$ fv MA web.mit.edu 617-253-4791

Rensselaer **$$$$$** v (midsized, town) NY rpi.edu 518-276-6216

Institutions specializing in business
(All are four-year, small, in or near a big city, accept some B– or even
C+ students, and use a quarter calendar.)

Don't forget about your local colleges. (Need ideas? See your counselor.)

Bentley College **$$$$** MA bentley.edu 800-523-2354

Bryant College **$$$$** RI bryant.edu 800-622-7001

Babson College (mainly B students or better) **$$$$$** MA babson.edu
800-488-3696

Institutions specializing in the visual arts
(Unless otherwise noted, all are four-year, small, in or near a big
city, and take about half of applicants, with special emphasis on the
portfolio.)

Don't forget about your local colleges. (Need ideas? See your counselor.)

North Carolina School of the Arts **$/$$$** t NC ncarts.edu
336-770-3291

Cooper Union (mainly A students) **$$** NY cooper.edu 212-353-4120

Fashion Institute of Technology (easier admission) **$/$$** NY fitnyc.edu
212-217-7675

Art Center College of Design **$$$$** (no room and board) lt CA artcen-
ter.edu 626-396-2373

Kansas City Art Institute **$$$$** MO kcai.edu 800-522-5224

Maryland Institute College of Art **$$$$** l MD mica.edu 410-225-2222

School of the Art Institute of Chicago (easier admission) **$$$$** IL
artic.edu/saic 800-232-SAIC

Otis College of Art & Design (easier admission) **$$$** CA otisarts.edu
800-527-OTIS

Parsons School of Design $$$$$ l NY parsons.edu 877-528-3321

Rhode Island School of Design $$$$ lf RI risd.edu 800-364-RISD

Institutions specializing in the performing arts

(Unless otherwise noted, all are four-year, small, suburban/urban, and take about half of applicants, with special emphasis on performing ability.)

Don't forget about your local colleges. (Need ideas? See your counselor.)

Curtis Institute of Music (most selective) $ (no room and board) PA curtis.edu 215-893-5252

Purchase College, State U. of NY $$/$$$ lq NY purchase.edu 914-251-6300

California Institute of the Arts lt (town) $$$$ CA calarts.edu 800-545-ARTS

Cleveland Institute of Music $$$$ q OH cim.edu 216-795-3107

Columbia College $$$ (IL) (easier admission) colum.edu 312-663-1600

Julliard (most selective) $$$$ q NY julliard.edu 212-799-5000 x223

Berklee College of Music $$$$ MA berklee.edu 800-237-5533

Eastman School of Music (very selective) $$$$ NY rochester.edu/eastman 800-292-3040

Manhattan School of Music $$$$$ q NY msmnyc.edu 212-749-2802, x2

Mannes College of Music $$$$$ q NY mannes.edu 800-292-3040

New England Conservatory $$$$$ q MA newenglandconservatory.edu 617-585-1101

Oberlin Conservatory $$$$$ f OH Oberlin.edu/con 440-775-8413

Appendix C

College Planning Calendar

Junior Year of High School

FALL & WINTER

- ✓ Get good grades. This year and the first half of next year are the most important for college admissions.

- ✓ Register in early September for the PSAT in October.

- ✓ Be sure you have a Social Security card. It's required for college applications.

- ✓ To get the maximum financial aid, money for college should be saved in the parent's name, not the student's. Where possible, family expenses should be paid with money that already is in the student's name. Capital gains should be taken by December 31 of your junior year. If your parents only put money aside for retirement in some years, the best time to do it is by December 31 of your junior year.

SPRING

- ✓ Select a tentative major (See pp. 208–215 for how.)

- ✓ Sign up for the May administration of the SAT or ACT.

- ✓ Develop a tentative list of colleges by completing Chapters 1 and 2 in this book. Involve your parents, but don't let them dominate.

- ✓ In June, if one or more of your target colleges require it, take three SAT II exams: math and your best two other subjects. (Forget about the latter if you took the SAT II: Biology at the end of your sophomore year.)

✓ If you're a "superstar," an "underrepresented" minority, or know that your family will not qualify for much financial aid, consider investigating private scholarships. A good free scholarship search service is at *wiredscholar.com*.

✓ Consider taking Advanced Placement exams.

✓ Create a filing system for college materials.

SUMMER

✓ Find or explore a passion. Not only will this be fun and perhaps help you find a career, it will enhance your college application. Keep a journal of your interesting experiences and insights. This will be useful in your college essay.

✓ Warning for those likely to qualify for financial aid: After the first $2,490 you earn and save each year, most colleges will reduce your financial aid by 50 to 85 cents for every dollar you earn. Consider that when deciding between a high-paying job or a meaningful low- or no-pay experience.

✓ Start work on your college admission essays. *The Fiske Guide to Colleges* lists recent essay topics for 300+ colleges.

✓ Decide how much to prepare for the SAT (or ACT). Get the books *10 Real SATs* and *Getting in the ACT*. Take one of their exams under timed conditions. If your score is up to 125 points too low on the old SAT (200 on the new SAT) for your target colleges, use Inside the SAT/ACT software to study.

✓ Go to each college's web site for admission and financial aid materials.

Senior Year of High School

SEPTEMBER

✓ If you haven't already taken the SAT or ACT, register for the October administration. The registration deadline is in early September.

- ✓ Keep your grades up. For many colleges, this is the most important semester.

- ✓ If you haven't already done so, use the techniques in Chapter 3 to narrow your list of colleges.

- ✓ If you expect to perform or play a varsity sport in college, have your coach contact the coaches at prospective colleges.

- ✓ If applying Early Decision or Early Action, give recommendation forms and your résumé to your recommenders.

OCTOBER

- ✓ If necessary, retake the SAT or ACT.

- ✓ Complete your applications; online is usually best. You can often save lots of time by using the Common Application (*www.commonapp.org*), which allows you to apply to as many as you like of 250 prominent colleges with one basic application.

- ✓ If you're applying Early Decision or Early Action, the deadline is coming up.

- ✓ Give recommendation forms and your résumé to your recommenders.

- ✓ Work on your essay(s).

- ✓ Check at each college's web site to find out which financial aid form(s) are required and the deadlines for filing.

NOVEMBER

- ✓ Remind recommenders of deadlines.

- ✓ Work on applications. Most deadlines for college applications aren't until later, but check to be sure!

DECEMBER

- ✓ Send off your applications before the deadline. If you're an athlete or performer, be sure to send a demo tape.

- ✓ Request transcripts to be sent to colleges requiring them.

- ✓ During vacation, complete any unfinished applications.

JANUARY/FEBRUARY

- ✓ Even if your family is well-off, apply for financial aid so you can be considered for merit-based scholarships. A must: Submit financial aid forms by the deadlines; you needn't wait until your parents have done their tax return. Check each college's financial aid web site for specifics.

- ✓ If you think you'd interview well or if an interview is required, request one at private colleges or with a local alumni interviewer.

- ✓ If your colleges require it, have your midyear grade transcripts sent.

SPRING

- ✓ Use the tips in Chapters 2 and 3 to confirm the colleges at which you are most likely to be happy and successful.

- ✓ Application deadlines for many Canadian and British universities are in May and June.

- ✓ Consider doing something nonacademic but substantive for a semester or a year before starting college (see pp. 64–66). Most colleges will let you do that. Just convince your college that you're taking the time off to do something substantial, not just sleep late.

- ✓ If you're unhappy with being wait-listed, with a financial aid award, or with a housing assignment, consider an appeal.

- ✓ Tell all the colleges that offered you admission where you've decided to enroll. Send in your housing form as soon as possible. Early birds often get the best housing. Latecomers may not get housing at all.

- ✓ Submit a final transcript to the college you've selected.

- ✓ Consider taking Advanced Placement exams.

✓ June 30, or your last day of high school enrollment, whichever comes first, is the deadline for submitting your SAR (Federal Financial Aid report) to your college's financial aid office.

✓ Be proud. You've completed a tough task!

SUMMER

✓ Develop or explore a passion. It may give you a greater sense of purpose as you begin college.

✓ Develop your game plan for making the most of the college you've selected. (See Chapter 6.)

✓ Pack for college.

✓ Leave home for your new home. Be your best self and have fun.

Appendix D

Application Deadline Form

College applications have more deadlines than a journalist. This will help you keep track. Write in each deadline. Check weekly to see which ones are coming up. Each time you meet one, cross it out.

	COLLEGE 1	COLLEGE 2	COLLEGE 3	COLLEGE 4	COLLEGE 5	COLLEGE 6	COLLEGE 7	COLLEGE 8
Your deadline for submitting the application *(Regular Action or Early Decision/Action/Admission)*								
Last date you can submit your SAT or ACT scores								
Last date you can submit your SAT II scores								
Deadline for submitting Advanced Placement test scores								
Deadline for submitting your transcript								
Deadline for submitting your mid-senior-year transcript								
Deadline for submitting your recommendations								
Deadline for filing the FAFSA								
Deadline for filing the Profile								
Deadline for filing any other required financial aid forms								
Deadline for informing colleges whether you'll attend								
Deadline for sending final transcript to your college								
Deadline for submitting AP test scores taken during second half of senior year								

Appendix E

Choosing a Career and a Major

Many students, parents, and counselors think it's a mistake to choose a career or major while still in high school. Their argument is that most high school students haven't had enough life experience to choose a career, and that they'll be exposed to much more in college.

Those arguments are outweighed:

✓ Tentatively choosing a career and major can help you choose a college—you can focus on colleges with strong programs in that major. Don't end up liking that major? No problem. Nearly all colleges offer dozens if not hundreds of majors you can switch to.

✓ If you choose your major carefully, you may avoid having to change majors, which can put you on the ever more popular six-year graduation plan.

✓ Settling on a career often takes time. Many people are still trying to figure out what they want to be when they grow up long after graduating college while their more planful peers (that means you) are forging ahead in their chosen career. High school is a great time to start the exploration process.

Choosing a Career

Here are six approaches to figuring out the answer to that annoying question, "What do you want to be when you grow up?"

Approach 1: Answer *The 19 Most Revealing Questions*
I ask my clients these questions to help them pick a career. **Expect that only a few of your answers will generate a useful clue.**

Questions to tease out the unusual in us

No one wants to feel ordinary. One way to feel special is to find a career that incorporates something unusual about you. That also may yield better pay because employers often pay more for rare attributes than for common ones.

1. What ability do you have that most people lack? One example: the ability to think quickly on your feet.

2. Do you have an unusual personality characteristic? One example: the ability to remain calm under pressure.

3. Do you believe something different from what most people believe? One example: that genetically engineering human intelligence is a good idea.

Questions to tease out career clues from daily life

4. What subject in school are you good at *and* like a lot?

5. What have people complimented you on?

6. What kinds of problems do you solve well in school? At home? One example: mediating fights between friends.

7. On what productive task, do you spend a lot of time while enjoying the process? Consider tasks done in school, after school, on weekends, and during the summer. One example: building models.

8. If I looked around your room, including through your drawers, what clue(s) might I learn about you? One example: if three health-related books sit alongside your bed, perhaps you might consider a health-related career.

9. What items do you save? One example: articles on a certain topic.

10. What do you find easy that many people find difficult?

11. Where do you picture yourself working: an office, at home, outdoors, a school?

Questions that look at our dark side

We're encouraged to think positive, act positive. Yet our dark side may offer career clues.

12. Is there a product that makes you so unhappy you'd like to do something about it?

13. Is there a service (one example: school) that makes you so unhappy you'd like to do something about it?

14. Is there an aspect of society that makes you so unhappy you'd like to do something about it?

15. What would be your job from hell? Would you like to do the opposite?

16. Which one or two are you:
      a word person
      a math/science person
      a people person
      an artistic person
      a fix-it/build-it person
      a paperwork details person

Question to identify a career angel

It is sad but true that who you know often counts as much as what you know.

17. Do you know a wealthy, well-connected, eminent, or highly skilled person who could open an interesting career door for you?

The most powerful questions

Sometimes, these questions are the most revealing of all.

18. What do you want? What do you really want?

19. What could keep you from getting it?

Now, look at your answers to the 19 questions. Pick out the one, two, or three clues that feel most significant. Does any career come to mind? Stuck? Ask family and friends to help.

If you come up with a career that sounds exciting, learn more about it by doing a search at google.com or by using the resources at *www.rileyguide.com/careers.html.*

Approach 2: Your Five Peaks

List five things you've done, in or out of school, that came out well, and that you enjoyed doing. For each, write a paragraph describing what you did. Is there an ability that you seem to use a lot? Do your paragraphs suggest a clue to what sort of career you might pursue? Not sure? Consider asking parents or friends.

Approach 3: Consider 500 Careers in an Hour!

Take this with a grain of salt—I'm recommending another book I wrote, *Cool Careers for Dummies*. It contains quick introductions (like those in Approach 6 below) to more than 500 careers and self-employment opportunities, covering 95 percent of all workers. You can browse it in an hour.

Approach 4: A Computer Program

Yes, these are the career "tests" that often generate weird recommendations, such as "clergy" even though you're an atheist. But more often than not, these programs offer valuable information. Your high school may offer one such as SIGI-Plus, Discover, or, in California, Eureka, which suggests careers and majors based on your skills, interests, and values. If your school doesn't have such a program, you can take the Campbell Skill and Interest Survey online for $17.95. The Campbell, like all these assessments, is far from perfect, but is well regarded by most career counselors. It's available online at *www.usnews.com/ usnews/edu/careers/ccciss.htm.*

Approach 5: The Family Approach

Your parent (or other relative) can teach you about their career. Of course, that's only one or two careers, but there are often reasons to consider one of them. Genetically, you are similar to your parents, your upbringing is probably similar, they are likely to teach you secrets on succeeding in that career that outsiders never get to hear, they can give you inside advice on how to prepare for that career and leads on good internships and jobs, and they can offer counsel once you're working in that field.

Approach 6: The Holistic Approach

Below are introductions to 26 careers popular among college graduates, plus 12 less well-known cool careers that many people find rewarding. To learn more about any of them, see the Occupational Outlook Handbook, available online at *www.bls.gov/oco*. For most of the careers, I also list a web site or book with more information.

WORD-CENTRIC CAREERS

Librarian. You work in a pleasant environment, helping people with usually solvable problems, and get to see the latest and sometimes greatest in books, magazines, and online resources. And unlike in most careers today, you rarely have to work overtime. With more and more content available online, librarians must be whizzes at digging up information on the computer. The money isn't great, but the quality of life is extraordinary.

Teacher. The good teacher's most important attributes: enthusiasm, ability to explain things clearly, and a knack for getting kids to like you and respect you. If they don't like you, at least some students will misbehave and it takes only a few to turn your classroom into a zoo, especially in schools serving disadvantaged students. One-third of teachers leave the profession within the first five years, mainly because they lack one of the above characteristics. If, however, you have the right stuff, teaching can be extremely rewarding. See Pearl Rock Kane's book, *The First Year of Teaching*.

Clergy. Except for having to be on call 24/7, this is a wonderful profession: high status, good pay, unmitigated do-gooding. Plus the opportunity to express your most profound thoughts in your sermons and meetings with individuals.

Writer. Many people (including your author) write because we feel we *must* write—we're compelled to share our ideas. Indeed, unless you feel compelled to write, write as a sideline, because the odds of making even a subsistence living as a writer are slim. That's especially true if your goal is to write the great American novel or screenplay. Most people who earn a living at writing are journalists, write ads or corporate documents, or write for a specialty publication such as *Pizza Today*. Most professional writers are not only good, but fast. A typical newspaper reporter researches and writes an article in just a few hours. Go to *Freelancewrite.about.com.*

Lawyer. You're not good in science and like to argue, so you figure you should become a lawyer, right? Not necessarily. The prestige is great, and *if* you're a graduate of a top law school, and doing corporate law, the money can be tops. But 75 percent of lawyers are unhappy; too much reading and writing boring, detailed documents, too much pressure, too many long hours, too much fighting—and over what? Usually which of two corporations should get more money. Myth: Law is a good option for people who want to cure social problems. Only a tiny percentage of lawyers end up with public interest jobs, and those are usually graduates of prestigious law schools and get paid a small fraction of what corporate lawyers earn. Law is an overrated career, but there are neat niches, such as adoption law and patent law. Go to *www.abanet.org.* and click on "career counsel."

Here are less well-known careers for word lovers:

✓ **Magazine Editor.** An editor chooses topics and writers. For example, "Let's do a story called 'Supermodels' Beauty Secrets'— I think Wanda Wordsmith would be a great person to write it." When Wanda submits a draft, a copy editor polishes it up before publication. For more information, visit *www.asme.magazine.org.*

✓ **Politician's Writer.** Every politician uses writers, from Podunk school board member to the president of the United States. Using a style that's a cross between journalist and ad writer, they craft speeches, fund-raising letters, and those vote-for-me postcards that stuff our mailboxes. For more information, visit *http://pcl.stanford.edu/.*

✓ **Ghostwriter.** Perhaps the most likely way to get to write a best seller is to be a ghostwriter. Publishers are eager to have famous people write books, but most of them can't write, so they hire a ghostwriter to write it. Almost always, the book's cover reads, "By [insert famous person's name] with [insert ghostwriter's name.] **Insider's Secret:** Both of Hillary Clinton's books, *It Takes a Village* and *Living History* were ghostwritten by Barbara Feinman Todd, yet both covers say only "By Hillary Clinton." No ghostwriter is mentioned.

PEOPLE-CENTRIC CAREERS

College Administrator. A college campus is a great place to work: beautiful environment, intelligent people, learning opportunities all around you, and work hours that tend to be shorter than in corporations. Administrators supervise such programs as student housing, minority recruitment, or computer services. Best place to start: when in college, get a student job in the college administration building.

Producer. This is a title you can bestow on yourself. It's basically anyone who tries to raise the money and find the talent to put on some sort of entertainment: a play, movie, concert, and so on. There's an old Hollywood joke: "What does it take to be a producer? Business cards." See John Lee's book, *The Producer's Business Handbook.*

Speech/Language Therapist. Think of how you feel when you listen to a stutterer. Imagine how he feels. The speech/language therapist treats stuttering and other voice and speaking problems You may work in a hospital, rehab center, or school. This is one of the few school-based careers in which you get to work one on one most of the day—very pleasant. The downside: your clients' progress is often slow. See *www.asha.org,* then click on "careers."

Salesperson. When you hear the word "salesperson," what's the first word that comes to mind? Pushy? Many successful salespeople don't fit the stereotype. They are, however, likeable self-starters, pleasantly persistent, good at listening to the customer (harder than you probably think) and good at explaining how a product can solve the customer's problems. Good salespeople aren't reluctant to ask for the sale, and don't fear rejection. Some people like knowing their income depends on their performance: the more you sell, the more you make. See Tom Hopkins's book, *Selling for Dummies.*

Self-employment. Finding secure employment will be ever more difficult. Among the most secure work may be to own a *simple* business, such as a small chain of espresso carts called The Uncorporate Café. Locate them opposite Starbucks. The simpler and more proven a business idea, the greater the chances of its success.

Fund-raiser. You persuade wealthy individuals and companies to donate big bucks to keep a nonprofit organization running. Fund-raisers also plan gala events or manage databases to boost donations. Go to *www.nsfre.org.*

Personal Coach. You help people set and keep goals related to career, school, relationships, health, and money. Unlike psychologists, who try to help people understand *why* they are the way they are, coaches focus mainly on solutions. Bonus: training is much shorter than for psychologists and other counselors. For more information, visit, *www.coachu.com.*

SCIENCE/MATH CAREERS

Biologist. I attended a presentation by five Nobel Prize winners. One of the few things they agreed on was that the field that would make the biggest difference in coming decades was molecular biology. You may end up doing much to improve the world: cure disease, create plants that don't need spraying with pesticide, figuring out what genes cause what characteristics. Imagine if we could end mental retardation! Most biologist jobs require you to be outstanding in math and with computers. For more information, visit *about.biology.com.* Then click on "students."

Engineer. This is the perfect career for those who like designing objects using science, math, and computers. Cool projects: creating a solar-powered car or a robot that will walk your dog while you're at work. The downside: engineering majors must take many courses, so it often takes five or more years to earn a bachelor's degree. Also, many engineers complain that they rarely use most of what they learned in school. One other downside: women engineers leave the field at twice the rate of men. Go to *www.nap.edu/readingroom/books/careers/contents.html*, or see Celeste Baines's book, *Is There an Engineer Inside You?*

Architect. The good news is that you get to design buildings. The bad news is that most architects don't get to design their first building until they're middle-aged. Most clients who can afford architects are older and don't trust young people. So young architects, after years of study, pay lots of dues designing such things as the ducting for a warehouse or ensuring that the senior architect's design meets the city's regulations. Go to *www.aia.org*.

Pharmacist. Your job is much more than counting out pills. You are a first-line health care provider: teaching diabetics how to inject themselves with insulin, helping people with their blood pressure monitoring, and perhaps most important, ensuring that patients know how to take their medications. This isn't as easy as it sounds. Many older people must take many medications, each of which must be taken at a different time, some of which must be taken on an empty stomach, others when not drowsy. As important, pharmacists ensure that drugs can be taken together safely. Pharmacists can be a lifesaver. Go to *www.aacp.org*, then click on "for students."

Genetic Counselor. Here's a typical example of what a genetic counselor does: A married couple both suffer from severe depression. They're thinking about having a child. A genetic counselor helps them understand the chances their child will suffer from depression, facilitates their decision whether to get pregnant, and helps them make peace with their decision. Go to *www.nsgc.org*, then click on "career."

Optometrist. "Better with lens A or lens B?" After a while, I can never tell and feel like a dunce. In any case, optometrists diagnose and treat eye conditions, usually by prescribing glasses or contact lenses. In some states, they can even do some minor surgery. Optometry is a particularly rewarding health career because it identifies significant problems that usually have a ready cure. Go to *www.aoanet.org* and click on "students and education."

Electrician. I'm shocked that more people aren't becoming electricians. It's less physically demanding than other blue-collar jobs yet is among the best paying. And surprisingly, electricians are seriously injured by electricity at only half the rate of the general population. Just don't be color-blind: All electric wires are color coded! Although you need a good brain—electricians spend a lot of time diagnosing problems and figuring out clever solutions—you don't need a college degree. You usually become an electrician through a four-year apprenticeship or by informal learning on the job. For more information, visit *http://www.bls.gov/oco/ocos206.htm.*

Physician. Although this career's prestige and salary are high, and it feels good to help people, this career has downsides. Your college education is exceptionally rigorous—fewer than one in four students who start college premed actually get into med school. And the education is long: four years of college, four years of med school, one to six years more of internship and residency. And you could well have $100,000 to $200,000 in student loans to pay back. Once you're a doctor, it's still no picnic. You're frequently in high-stakes situations; for example, a misdiagnosis can be devastating. And there's the pressure to see more patients in less time, ever more of whom—thanks to the Internet—may know more about their condition than you do. Neat niches: infectious diseases, infertility. See Marita Danek's book, *Becoming a Physician.*

Physical Therapist. Typical physical therapy patients: a plumber who injured his back, a person recovering from a stroke, an infant with a birth defect. The therapist devises programs, usually including exercises, to speed recovery. Many people think physical therapists coach the patient through exercises, but in many cases, that's done mainly by poorly paid physical therapy aides. Go to *www.apta.org*, then click "careers."

Accountant. Do you like order and detail? Are you happy around numbers? Accounting may be for you. But to get ahead, you need good communication skills. Downside: one of an accountant's main jobs is to impart bad news: "No, you can't do that." Or "I need better documentation of that." Accountants seem always in demand, not just by individuals or companies, but by the government.

Programmer. Programmers start with a real-world problem, such as how to monitor the amount of electricity Minnesota uses per second. They figure out how that can be calculated and then use a programming language to "teach" the computer how to calculate it. That part, for really bright people, tends to be challenging, fun, and addictive. But after the basic program is written, major tedium usually follows. Debugging often means days of staring at screenfuls of numbers and letters, trying to divine which ones are wrong.

Here are less well-known careers for science/math types:

✓ **Statistician.** You do math to figure out questions like the following: Four of 100 patients who tried a new drug suffered headaches, whereas only two who took a placebo got a headache. Did that occur by chance, or does the drug, in fact, cause headaches? Go to *www.amstat.org.*

✓ **Physician's Assistant.** Training is much shorter than to become an MD, yet you get to do many of doctors' most rewarding tasks: wellness exams and health education. Visit *www.aapa.org.*

✓ **Toxicologist.** You get to figure out how to deal with air and water pollution, and biological and chemical weapon attacks. Go to *www.toxicology.org.*

ARTISTIC CAREERS

Filmmaker. What could sound cooler than "Hi, I'm a feature filmmaker"? Beyond sounding cool, directing feature films *is* cool. You get to orchestrate the telling of a story that you put in front of thousands of viewers. And the process is the ultimate in creativity and camaraderie, with you leading your film crew in working intensely for months, until it's finished. Then, you can sit back and watch your masterpiece and see the money roll in. What a dream! Unfortunately, for 99.99 percent of aspiring filmmakers, it is only a dream. Even many graduates of the top film schools (University of California, Los Angeles and University of Southern California) end up never earning enough to pay back their student loans, let alone earning a subsistence living as a filmmaker. Nevertheless, if my daughter said, "Dad, I want to be a filmmaker," I would not discourage it—the prospect is just too exciting. I'd rationalize that if she couldn't make it as a filmmaker in Hollywood, she could somehow make a living creating training videos. See *www.aivf.org*, then click on "resources for indies."

Actor. The good news is that the job market may be improving a bit. With the proliferation of Internet video for entertainment and training, and increased cable and satellite viewership, the need for actors is increasing. But there's plenty of bad news. Eighty percent of actors in the Screen Actors Guild (those who have already acted in a union job) earn less than $5,000 a year from their acting! Even the term "actor" is misleading. It implies you're acting, doing something. For the most part, actors wait. They wait to be hired. Once hired, on the set, they wait for their turn, for the weather to clear, for the technoids to set things up, for the producer, director, and minions to make up their minds. Acting as a hobby—for example, acting in volunteer community theater productions—is a great way to get on stage while avoiding most of an acting career's downsides. See Robert Cohen's book, *Acting Professionally: Raw Facts About Careers in Acting.*

Artist. If you have visions of hanging out in your loft, splattering paint on some enormous canvas, congratulations—you have a cool hobby. The Princeton Review profile of artist careers reports that "as a purely self-expressing career, 90 percent of artists make under $1,000 per year on their art." If you expect to make a living as an artist, brand this into your brain: seventy-five percent of the art available in the United States is produced by the advertising industry. Much of the rest appears on web sites. And almost all is computer-generated art produced by people with excellent freehand drawing skills.

Interior Designer. What fun! Helping people figure out how to make their homes or offices beautiful and functional. And you get to go on shopping sprees. Trouble is, if you expect to make a living, the job usually requires much more than that: reading blueprints, creating estimates for commercial and residential projects, developing mockups using computer-aided design systems, and knowing whether you can knock down a wall without the building collapsing. In short, you're somewhere between a decorator and an architect. Go to *www.asid.org* and click on "careers."

Landscape Architecture. Preserving Yosemite Park, designing the U.S. Capitol grounds, creating Boston's "Emerald Necklace" of green spaces tying the city to the suburbs. Landscape architecture is a career for architect types who are interested in outdoor design. Projects can be mundane, like designing the spaces between buildings in an industrial park or building an artificial pond in a homeowner's backyard. Or they can be exotic like designing the landscapes of resorts, golf courses, zoos, urban plazas, colleges, cemeteries, landmark monuments, or scenic highways. See *www.asla.org.*

Here are less well-known options for artistic types:

✓ **Newborn Photographer.** It amazes me that life's most inspiring event, childbirth and the day after, is rarely photographed professionally. Try to get a hospital director to allow you to offer your service to expectant parents who will be giving birth at the hospital. Go to *www.ppa-world.org.*

✓ **Trade Show Exhibit Designer.** In most industries, companies assemble each year to show their wares to customers. Each company has a booth, and it has to attract attention. Someone's got to design those booths. Want to be that person? Go to *www.edpa.com.*

✓ **Costume Designer.** You study a TV or movie script, then create or buy clothes that are appropriate to the story's period for the actors to wear on the set. See *www.costumedesignguild.com.*

✓ **Visual Effects Designer.** Take your skills as an artist and enhance them with computers to create visual wonders for video games and movies, like making someone's curly black hair instantly turn straight and blonde. Go to *pixar.com/FAQs.html*.

Now What?

If you've identified a career of interest:

✓ Read about it at the suggested web site, in the *Occupational Outlook Handbook* (*www.bls.gov/oco*), material in your high school's career center, and/or from a google.com search.

✓ Talk with people in that career, ideally at their place of work. Sometimes your parents may know someone in the field. If you have guts, call people out of the Yellow Pages. You'll be surprised how willing most people are to talk about their careers, especially with a high school student.

✓ Do a term paper on a career-related issue. Your teacher may let you do that instead of the regularly assigned topic.

✓ Visit your college's career center. It may help you get leads on a job or help you find a co-op program or summer internship that would put you at the elbow of someone employed in your target career. You'll get a better sense of whether you really want to pursue that career. One girl thought she wanted to be a veterinarian until she volunteered in a vet's office, whereupon she realized she liked well animals but not sick ones.

Choosing a Major

Start by scanning the one-paragraph descriptions of each of 600 majors in the *Index of Majors and Graduate Degrees*. (It's produced by the College Board and revised annually.) Within an hour, you'll have discovered many options you've never considered. Ever think of majoring in enology (wine making), virology (viruses), recreational therapy, playwriting, oceanography, museum studies, geronotology (aging), forensics (how to analyze criminal evidence)? Don't like those? *The Index of Majors and Graduate Degrees* describes 592 more.

Learn more about majors of interest at *www.ksu.edu/acic/career/options.html* or by going on an Internet search for that career.

Those strategies tend to yield scrupulously neutral information. Here are my more subjective impressions of three dozen popular majors based on discussions with hundreds of people, young and old. My focus here is on correcting misconceptions or presenting important information that rarely finds its way into print.

LIBERAL ARTS MAJORS

Art History. A graduate degree is required to stand a chance of getting sought-after jobs, such as those in in museums, historic preservation, or archiving.

Biology. If you think that studying biology means learning about cute endangered species, forget it. For the most part, college biology (and its related fields biochemistry and biophysics) is math. Many students find the major difficult and boring; that's not a great combination. There's an oversupply of biology Ph.D.s, so most job openings are for bachelor's degree holders. Unfortunately, many bachelor's-level jobs allow little autonomy. To go to medical school, you needn't major in biology; you only need one year of biology (plus two years of chemistry, a year of physics, and (God knows why) a year of calculus.

Black, Latino, Women's, or American Studies. Many students enjoy these majors and find them empowering, but they can raise red flags to employers. These majors have little relevance to the work most employers are hiring for, and can make you hypersensitive to perceived slights.

Design Your Own Major. The upside is that you get to study what you care about. The downside is that most employers won't know what to make of your major, and therefore, in a tough job market, may drop your resume into the circular file.

English (literature emphasis). If you loved literature in high school, you'll probably love it in college. However, in college, the emphasis is often on interpreting literature primarily through one lens: race/class/gender.

English (creative writing emphasis). One of the most enjoyable majors—alas, one that, in most fields, doesn't boost your chances of employment.

Economics. This is not a near-business major and employers won't think it is. Also, don't let the Intro to Economics course fool you: this is a math-centric major.

Environmental Studies. Unless the program has a strong science emphasis, you won't learn much that will impress employers. You will, however, grow to care deeply about protecting flora and fauna.

Foreign Language. Major in a Middle Eastern or African language, and you may find yourself with job offers in all sectors: government, nonprofit, corporations.

A Spanish major, if focused on communication rather than literature, will also put you in demand.

History. Another of the more enjoyable and well-taught majors. No, it doesn't open many career doors, but if you're headed for law school, medical school, or business school, it doesn't matter. They'll all welcome history majors, indeed all liberal arts majors.

International Relations. This is enjoyable because you get to study a little of everything: political science, history, sociology, plus a few courses about a region of interest. Alas, this is also the major's greatest weakness. International relations can easily cause the imposter syndrome: the sense that, even though you have a degree, you don't know much about anything.

Liberal Studies. This is another major for dabblers. Liberal studies majors take one or two courses in a number of liberal arts fields.

Math. For the person who intuitively understands math and appreciates its elegance, math is an outstanding major. It is a building block for many graduate programs and for careers as diverse as biostatistics, stock market picking, and cryptography (deciphering coded messages.)

Music Appreciation. Tops for pleasure, bottom for enhancing employability. It's an easy major—most music courses don't require you to read a stack of fat books. "Listen to Beethoven's Ninth and Manhattan Transfer, then compare and contrast." Now, that's a fun assignment.

Philosophy. Here's where my practical self wimps out a bit. My fondest memories of my undergraduate days are of taking a philosophy course. I don't remember most of what I learned, but I somehow have the sense that it has made me a more thoughtful person. Of course, don't think of a philosophy major as a career door opener. Plan on graduate school or self-employment, or do summer internships to pave the way for future employment.

Physics. I attended a panel discussion among five Nobel–prize winning scientists. They agreed that physics' heyday was over and that this will be the century of molecular biology and genetics.

Political Science. This is another major that many students enjoy enough that they're willing to accept that it may not help them land a job. It's a mistake to think you need to major in political science if you're planning to go to law school. Law schools routinely admit majors in everything from agriculture to zoology.

Psychology (physiological focus). This is the wave of the future. Scientists are discovering that more and more psychological problems have physiological roots. But we're far from being fully able to use this knowledge to help people. If you're interested in a research career, this is a terrific field.

Psychology (traditional focus). Twenty-five years from now, traditional psychology will likely be viewed as alchemy. It's fun to read about theories of psychological development and functioning, but too rarely does that knowledge translate into practices that help people significantly. Most therapists succeed by trusting gut instinct rather than the theories they learned in college or graduate school.

Sociology. Like traditional psychology, this is a field that is not substantive: a lot of unproven theory made to look scientific by applying statistics to it. Ultimately, much of what you're taught in sociology simply reflects the political biases (almost always liberal) of the instructor.

CAREER-SPECIFIC MAJORS

Agriculture. If you like the idea of being involved in that most elemental of needs—providing food for people—and like the idea of an outdoor career that blends science with business, an agriculture major is worth considering.

Art (studio). A fun major. Alas, only a tiny, tiny percent of art majors ever end up earning enough money from their art to pay back their student loans, let alone earn a living. So, if you have visions of supporting yourself by painting canvases in your loft, you face lottery odds—unless you're very talented *and* a great marketer.

Business—Accounting. The job market is strong, and people who enjoy the black-and-white clarity of numbers may enjoy accounting. But many accountants, including my best friend, find that after a while, you begin to question whether there might be a more meaningful way to spend your work life than crunching numbers.

Business—Entrepreneurship. As U.S. companies downsize to the bone and export many jobs to places such as India, one of the last bastions of job security is self-employment. Yes, most entrepreneurs go out of business, but if you first learn the art and science of entrepreneurship, and are a good practical problem solver and not a procrastinator, you may find yourself, at age 22, being the CEO of a successful company from which you can never be fired.

Business—Management. The United States has 35 million managers, many of whom are not happy. They often feel caught between trying to meet their boss's overly optimistic expectations and playing slavedriver and cop to supervisees. Increasing numbers of managers reject this vise and return to roles as individual contributors.

Computer Science. Over the long haul, this major should serve the brilliant, analytical person well. There will always be the need for better hardware and software, with applications to all areas of business and home. For example, biotech companies hire many computer scientists to help devise better ways to identify which genes and proteins cause what reactions in which people.

Criminal Justice. Alas, crime will always be with us, and therefore we will have an ongoing need for law enforcement officers and employees of the court and penal systems. I would not want to spend my life dealing with lawbreakers, but some people find it compelling.

Education. The education major tends to be easy, some say boring—not much more than common sense plus theories that have little applicability to the classroom.

Engineering. Most engineering jobs require someone who'd rather spend all day interacting with a computer than with people. Yes, to rise among the ranks, you need communication skills, but for every chief there are usually a dozen supervisees whose jobs don't require them to say much.

Film/Television Studies. This enjoyable major helps you critique the media, usually through colleges' favorite lens: race/class/gender. It also teaches you the important art of story creation and allows you to explore life's universal themes of love, ambition, revenge, redemption, and so forth. Careers in the film and TV world are viewed as exciting and glamorous, so to succeed, you must be an impressive person and a prodigious networker.

Film/Television/Radio (hands-on). This major teaches you how to run film and TV equipment. I am not a fan of this major. Increasing numbers of the jobs in this field are being automated, and remaining positions will be tough to get and usually poorly paid. Many people choose this major in hopes of becoming on-air talent. Most on-air talents don't major in film/TV. The newsreaders, for example, are usually just pretty faces who can read a Teleprompter. On-air people whose gig requires them to think on their feet are selected because of their quick mind and (unfairly) their attractiveness, not their ability to run equipment. You can learn that on the job quickly.

Journalism. This is an enticing field. It's a career that can make a difference, you get to learn new things all the time, it's high status, and the working conditions and hours are good. If you can write well and on tight deadlines, consider journalism. But it's a crowded field, so your first jobs probably won't be in a big market. Think rural Midwest. The media is overwhelmingly liberal and sorely in need of conservatives. Alas, many people in the media don't think so—their commitment to balanced reporting is just talk.

Music Performance. When I entered college, I was already a professional musician and tried being a music major. I couldn't believe how the courses managed to excise the pleasure from music. Music theory didn't begin to enhance my appreciation of music let alone improve my musicianship. If you enjoy being a musician, in my opinion, take private lessons from a great teacher and major in something else.

Nursing. Jobs are expected to be plentiful for registered nurses. This is a stressful career but one that, for a caring, detail-oriented person, can be among the most rewarding. It also offers a wide range of opportunities: from obstetrics to hospice, patients' homes to hospitals. Top nurses often become nurse trainers, nurse practitioners, and nurse anesthetists.

Occupational Therapy. Occupational therapists help people regain practical life skills: help a stroke patient relearn to drive, find an alternative for an arthritis patient who can no longer button a shirt, and so on. The job market is expected to stay strong.

Optometry. Optometrists examine eyes and fit people for glasses and contact lenses. This is one of the most rewarding health careers because you succeed with the vast majority of your patients. And there's no blood and guts. Training, however, is long—typically seven years.

Pharmacy. The job market is expected to remain strong. Downsides: lots of night and weekend work, especially during your first years. Also, the required Doctor of Pharmacy degree takes six years.

Social Work. If you like the idea of counseling people, this is one of the shorter routes. In many states, a bachelor's from an accredited program will do. But you have to be able to be vulnerable enough to be caring but not so vulnerable that you burn out from all the clients with a constellation of hard-to-solve problems.

Theater. I love this major even though it offers scant employment potential. It helps you appreciate great literature at the same time as you get to participate in plays. That teaches you poise, public speaking, and teamwork, and is great fun. I've never seen as much camaraderie as among a play's cast and crew.

Now what?

Based on the above and the tentative career you selected in Appendix E, select a major. If you know you'll go to graduate school (70 percent say they will, but only 20 percent actually do), it isn't as important for you to choose a career-related major; you can do that in graduate school. If, however, you suspect you might not go to grad school, consider a career-related major such as engineering, business, nursing, or teacher education, or at least take some career-related courses.

Then find out which of the 10 to 15 colleges on your prospect list offer that major and read about it on one or more of those colleges' web sites. If none of your 10 to 15 colleges offers that major or a related one and you really want that major, consult the *Index of Majors and Graduate Degrees* to find colleges that offer it.

In your first term at college, take the introductory course in your prospective major. Don't let one course sway you too much. The rest of the major could be quite different.

Appendix F

Sure You Want to Go Straight to College?

A question you may not want to think about: **Are you sure you want to go straight from high school to college?** Next to a home, college is the biggest purchase most families ever make. And it's an expense that requires four to six years of your time, not to mention years of paying back loans.

Today, college is too often viewed as a magic pill, the solution to every clueless high school senior's problem. So you need to make sure that you're going to college because it's right for you, not because of the hype.

Here are three students who aren't sure they want to go straight to college, and what I have to say to them.

Student #1: "I'm not much of a student. I mainly get Cs and only got an 850 on the SAT (17 on the ACT). But almost everyone's going to college and my parents are pushing me to go. Should I?"

If college *prep* courses have been a struggle, actual four-year college courses may be overwhelming. Fewer than one in five college students with your high school grades and test scores get their bachelor's degree even if they take six years. Now, the good news. Even without a two-year degree, you needn't be stuck with a McJob. Many good career and life paths *don't* require a college degree. These days, you can launch a successful career by apprenticing with a webmaster, learning how to repair high-tech equipment in the military, or completing a resort management program at a community college. (Can you picture yourself in Hawaii?) For more information on un-college options, visit your high school's career center or counselor, or ask your family and friends about their jobs. Interested in an apprenticeship? You can use an apprenticeship to prepare for more than 800 careers—mainly working with your hands. To find your state's apprenticeship web site, go to *www.nastad.net* and click on "links." Look in the government section in the front of your nearest big-city White Pages and you'll find a listing for a local, state, or federal agency in charge of apprenticeships.

Student #2: *"I'm smart enough for college, but I'm sick of school. If I go to college, I just might goof off, especially because my parents won't be there to bug me."*

To keep your options open, apply to colleges. While you're waiting to hear from them, plan a time-out semester or year to do something real-world before starting college. For example, how about working in a hospital? Apprenticing with a master guitarmaker? Teaching an illiterate adult to read? Or all of these. (For more time-out ideas, see pp. 64–66.)

When you're accepted to a college, you can either say that you'll enroll right away or ask the college to hold your place for a semester or even a year. Most colleges will say yes.

Student #3: *"I could do fine at college, but I'd rather start my own business or try to get a decent job."*

Today, many people think you're a loser if you don't go to college. College is a must for most good students, but not for all. Don't fall for the line, "People who go to college earn more money than those who don't." They do make more money, but college isn't the main reason. College-bound students, on average, are more able and motivated than other students.

Even if college-bound people never actually went to college and were locked in a closet for the four years, they'd probably end up, on average, earning more money.

Especially if they're entrepreneurial, brilliant, persistent, or have family connections, some people do succeed without a college degree, for example: seven U.S. presidents from George Washington to Harry Truman, Domino's Pizza founder Tom Monaghan, Bill Gates, Quentin Tarantino (director of *Pulp Fiction*), Tony Robbins (success guru and consultant to the Clintons), Barbra Streisand, ABC-TV's Peter Jennings, Wendy's founder Dave Thomas, Thomas Edison, Blockbuster Video president Wayne Huizenga, Ernest Hemingway, McDonald's founder Ray Kroc, Henry Ford, Helena Rubenstein, Walt Disney, Ben Franklin, Alexander Graham Bell, John D. Rockefeller, Malcolm X, Apple Computer founder Steve Jobs, and thousands of other computer whizzes.

These folks did their learning at what I call *You U.*, by reading books, taking one-day seminars and individual courses, apprenticing with talented people, learning a lot on the job, and on the Internet. If you're confident you can succeed without college, you will avoid four to six years of school, save your family tons of money, and get a big head start on your career. You may even learn much more because you've crafted a completely individualized program, filled with hands-on learning and teachers that you've hand-picked from a variety of schools and workplaces. Many students graduate from college and lament that they remember very little of what they learned in their classes.

But before chucking college, hold on. The un-college option is a risky one. Many employers insist on a bachelor's degree. Also, more and more jobs require high-level math and science skills, which may be easier to acquire in college than on your own. Before deciding not to apply to college, talk with people in the fields you find exciting and see what opportunities exist without college. You don't want to end up in a career in which the most intelligent question you ever ask is, "Paper or plastic?"

And remember one very important thing. College is not just for career preparation, it's for—pardon my sounding like a parent—life preparation. (And, of course, for meeting fabulous men or women.) College usually improves your writing, speaking, and thinking skills, increases your knowledge and appreciation of the arts and sciences, and, in general, makes you a more thoughtful human being.

In sum, if you can handle the work, you probably should go to college. But don't get caught up in the everyone-goes-to-college fad. Choose college only if it's right for you.

I welcome your comments for the next edition. Write me at *mnemko@earthlink.net.*

Index

at home, 102
on-campus housing, 100–101
rooming with friend, 103
at two-year colleges, 150–151
Living-Learning Program, 160–161

M

Major:
choosing of, 195, 208–216
quality of, 29
switching of, 142
types of, 209–216
Mathematics careers, 202–205
Mental health counselors, 143–144
Mentor, 120, 127–128
Military academies, 90, 185
Mind-set, 67

N

National Association for College
Admission Counseling, 63–64
Net worth, 87
Newspapers, 15
Note-taking:
during campus visits, 26–27
during college, 135–136

O

On-campus housing, 100–101
Open house, 23
Orientation, 103

P

Parents:
application completion, 71–72
concerns by, 38
contributions by, 85–86
costs to, 21
deducting of expenses, 95
expectations of, 73
financial aid, 82

529 Savings Plan, 81
saving by, 80–81
visits by, 23
Part-time jobs, 93
People-centric careers, 201–202
PEP, 89
Performers, 59–60
Performing arts schools, 187
Personal appearance, 62
Physical sciences schools, 185–186
Picture-taking, 27
Planning calendar, 188–192
Pledging, 124
Plus Loans, 88
Power seats, 133–134
Prepping for tests, 136–139
Private colleges, 77–80, 95
Private scholarships, 87–88
Procrastination, 71, 108–110
Professional organizations, 121–122
Professors, 29, 96, 126–129
Public colleges, 76, 78–79

Q

Questions:
to admission counselors, 19
to fraternities, 125
general types of, 30–31
to sororities, 125
to students, 28
during visits, 30–32

R

Reading selections, 133
Recommendations, 55–56
Recommenders, 55–56
Rejection, 63–64
Religious colleges, 164
Resentment of authority, 110
Romantic life, 114–116
Roommate, 110–112
ROTC, 90